Billion Dollar IP Strategy

Intellectual Property for Tech CEOs, Unicorn Founders & Investors

By Raymond J. Hegarty

First edition ©2019

Second edition © 2024 Raymond J. Hegarty

Contents

Contents 2

Introduction 3

Prologue 9

Chapter 1 – Why IP strategy is different for billion-dollar companies 13

Chapter 2 – 5 steps to build an IP strategy 18

Chapter 3 – Intangible value and its components 32

Chapter 4 – Patents 41

Chapter 5 – Invention mining and the patenting process 52

Chapter 6 – How patents are enforced 59

Chapter 7 – Patent strategies 67

Chapter 8 – Trademarks 78

Chapter 9 – Trademark Strategies 84

Chapter 10 – Trade secrets 91

Chapter 11 – Trade secret strategies 101

Chapter 12 – Recognising intangibles in accounting terms . 111

Epilogue – IP strategy evolution 120

The last word 134

Author Profile 136

Introduction

People often think that intellectual property (IP) is the domain of lawyers.

That is like thinking that cars should only be driven by motor mechanics.

In the world of fast-growing technology companies, the bulk of corporate value is usually in intangible assets like intellectual property. If you, as CEO, are ultimately responsible for value creation, your responsibility is inseparable from the management of the risks and opportunities related to those intangible assets.

Of course, you don't need to become an IP lawyer. You just need to have the tools as CEO to ensure company's IP strategy is aligned with, and supporting, your corporate strategy.

That is the purpose of this book. It is aimed at busy executives who want a book that is short enough to read during a single flight and gain a better understanding of how to manage their intellectual property.

What this book is about

For billion-dollar technology companies, the value of intangible property is critical, yet IP value-maximization and risk abatement strategies are often neglected in the early years of development. This neglect can create problems in later years that are difficult and expensive to remedy and may even be fatal to the business.

This book focuses on the practical challenges faced by technology executives in harnessing and protecting intangible value. It first explains how to capture and protect intellectual property, and then provides guidance on what to do with the IP.

The objective is to help CEOs craft and execute strategies to:

- Enhance intangible value
- Eliminate IP risks

By doing so, CEOs will be able to focus on what matters – running their business and scaling for success.

What this book is not about

This book does not cover the minute details of filing and registering intellectual property. That is something that you should do in conjunction with qualified attorneys who undergo years of training to become specialised and licensed in this area.

Why should you buy this book?

This book is not designed to make you a patent attorney or patent specialist. It deliberately avoids legalistic details to focus on the business aspects of IP. It is aimed at educating you to be able to ask questions and understand what the professionals are talking about; allowing you to keep them focused on delivering the elements of the IP strategy that support your business aims in the most cost-effective way.

This book is for CEOs of high-growth technology companies. It deals with the intangible value of IP that is crucial for founders of companies with billion-dollar aspirations. It is also a useful guide for investors in those companies.

Variations in legal systems

Intellectual property protection is based in national legal systems. These systems have evolved over centuries to the modern versions we experience today. In the spirit of global cooperation and compatibility, there have been attempts to harmonise key aspects of respective national patent laws. However, differences remain. For example, patentable subject matter has different rules in the USA, Europe and China. Enforcement of trade secrets continues to evolve and is protected in different ways depending on where in the world breaches occur.

This book does not focus on one patent regime or another, but it does employ general concepts using local examples. Because the largest concentration of IP value for tech companies is based in the USA, American examples are more prevalent. And because IP is global, you will be introduced to key international aspects.

Why dollars?

Why does the book talk about a billion dollars? Why not Euro or Yen or Yuan?

The answer is that the world of IP thinks in dollars. Despite the huge interest in IP in Asia, the biggest value in IP is still in the USA. Where global licensing transactions are priced regionally, the USA portion of the deal usually is priced at a much higher royalty rate, whereas China is at the lowest rate and the "rest of world" is priced somewhere in between.

And, while there has been rapid growth in the number of Chinese unicorns in the past 5 years, the USA still boasts the highest number and valuations of current unicorn companies. Indeed, the definition of a unicorn firm is with reference to a billion-dollar-plus valuation.

For people who still prefer to think in terms of their regional currency, a billion dollars is of the same order of magnitude as a billion Euro, 100 billion Yen or 7 billion Yuan.

How to use this book

The book will take you through the most relevant areas quickly. It focuses on 3 key areas of intellectual property: patents, trademarks, and trade secrets. It gives guidance on how to mine for previously hidden value, identify it, capture it, protect it and use it as a source of competitive advantage.

The first chapter describes the framework that guides identifying gaps and protecting intellectual property on the way to enhancing intangible value. This sets the context for the chapters that follow which describe the key forms of intellectual property that are relevant for tech CEOs: how to protect it, the filing strategies to follow and how to exploit it.

The final part of the book examines how to use these intangible assets to enhance corporate value and address IP risks.

Disclaimer

This book is a general and informal overview of aspects of the business of intellectual property. It should not be taken in any way as, and is specifically not, providing legal or tax advice. You have not retained me. It is unlikely I have even met you.

As the author, I am not making any claims or inferences about results you may or may not achieve. This book is not a substitute for legal or financial advice. Before you make any decision, please engage professional advisors.

Special thank you

I am grateful for everyone who has worked with me to enrich my understanding of IP strategy.

I would like to especially thank the innovative and thoughtful Brian Seidman for his careful review of my drafts. He found my most glaring errors in the text and challenged me to refine my ideas and deliver more clarity.

I would also like to thank Donal O'Connell, an authority on trade secrets and IP risk, for his valuable comments and suggestions.

Despite their generous input, any errors that remain are entirely my responsibility.

I am particularly grateful to Alan O'Herlihy, who applied his design team to coming up with a cover for this book. Alan is inspirational as CEO of Everseen, an amazing high-growth AI innovation engine that is generating new world-class IP continuously.

Continue the conversation

The intention of this book is to give an overview of the world of intellectual property. If you would like to continue the conversation, you can get more detail on the IntaVal website at www.intaval.com or reach out to the author on social media.

Prologue

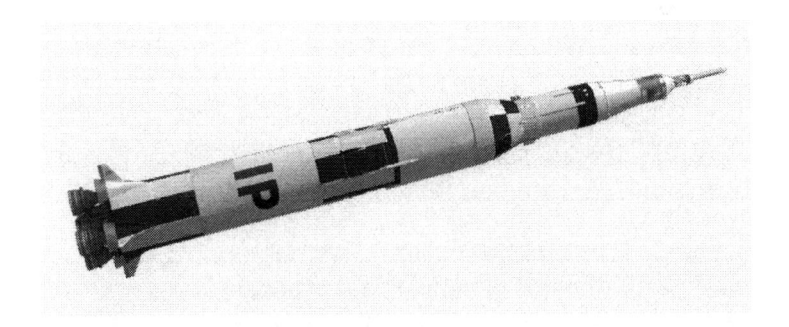

Achilles

In Greek mythology, Achilles was a fearsome warrior in the Trojan War who was believed to be invincible. He was the central character and greatest warrior in Homer's *Iliad*, and his heroic exploits have been retold in many dramatic works.

When Achilles was a baby, Princes Thetis – his mother – held him by the ankle and immersed him completely in the River Styx to give him the magical power of immortality.

However, because his mother's hand covered his ankle when she held him in the mythical river, just one part of his body was not blessed with the power of immortality. Achilles' heel was exposed as his only point of weakness.

The boy Achilles grew up to be a fearsome warrior. He won battles against valiant enemies and was central in the battle for Troy.

Near the end of the Trojan War, Achilles was killed by Paris with an arrow through his heel.

The Achilles Heel for tech companies

How is this relevant for a modern CEO?

Being a CEO of a tech company is a heady position. CEOs must deal with rapid growth and face sudden shifts in multiple dimensions. In this juggling act of prioritising resources and attention, IP can sometimes be left behind.

When the business is charging ahead, the CEO can feel like an invincible warrior. However, just like Achilles, a gap in IP strategy may be fatal for the business.

Ignoring IP may seriously disrupt a business. Here are some examples:

- It becomes more and more difficult to collaborate with partners and customers without first negotiating a non-disclosure agreement (NDA).
- Industry players may not take you seriously if you don't have a robust IP position.
- Without formal IP protection, it will be almost impossible to raise external funding.
- When inventions and personal contributions are not recognised, creative employees may become demoralised.

When the value of a fast-growing tech company is based almost entirely on intellectual property, ignoring IP and the lack of an IP strategy may be fatal. Here are some examples:

- Departing employees can take key trade secrets and bring them to a rival company.
- A merger negotiation regarding a software company may collapse during due diligence if their policy around the use of open-source software introduces a risk of infringing other companies' copyrights or patents.
- A firm's IPO may be derailed if they are accused in an unfortunately timed patent infringement case. Such a case exposing the firm to a risk that runs to hundreds of millions of dollars would spell doom for the launch.

Just a lucky shot?

One question arises from the story of Achilles. For such a great warrior, it seems such a random way to be killed when struck with an arrow in the heel. Was it just a lucky shot?

The story of the *Iliad* finishes without recounting the death of Achilles. However, later versions of the tale say that the arrow that Paris released was guided by the god Apollo who knew about the secret weakness.

Similarly, in business, a fatal blow may often be directed by a deliberate strategy where sophisticated rivals seek out areas of vulnerability in IP strategy and exploit those weaknesses deliberately.

This book aims to identify the most obvious weaknesses in IP strategy, address those weaknesses and place your company on a solid footing to capitalise on innovative opportunities.

Chapter 1 – Why IP strategy is different for billion-dollar companies

Becoming a billion-dollar firm is a goal for many tech entrepreneurs. Achieving scale is not merely a matter of vanity. Larger companies can take advantage of economies of scale and economies of scope. They can benefit from market power which boosts profitability and enhances survivability. Larger companies can influence industries and even national policy. Being the market leader in a "hot" industry gives a clear advantage in attracting and retaining key talent.

On the other hand, there are significant challenges that distinguish high-growth companies in terms of intangible value and IP strategy. Some of these challenges are highlighted in the sections below.

The largest part is intangible

The best high-growth technology companies start out as a combination of a market need, a novel solution and a great team to execute. The highest-profile ones follow a typical "hockey stick" growth. Initially starting slowly until they reach an inflection point, after which they accelerate on an upward trajectory.

When they are on this path to a billion-dollar valuation, the value of the company is not tied up in land, buildings and machinery, but in intellectual property.

And, since the value is primarily intangible, there is a clear vulnerability, especially if three factors are combined – the company is growing rapidly, the risks are not managed and the organisation lacks an effective IP strategy underpinning the future direction of the business.

Investors demand protection

TV reality shows such as "Shark Tank" or "Dragons' Den" feature entrepreneurs seeking investment from established entrepreneurs/investors. When they are questioned on their pitches, inevitably the entrepreneurs are asked how the idea is protected. If the idea is not protected completely, they need to demonstrate that they have a plan to address the gaps. If an investment offer is made, it will be conditional on the necessary protections being put in place.

That is TV. In the real world of venture capital, the amount of investor money at stake is orders of magnitude higher than what is available on the TV shows. The investors are more sophisticated. The pitches are more sophisticated.

Because the VCs have numerous opportunities pitched at them, they can afford to be more selective and discerning. VCs proudly reject almost every opportunity that is presented to them. Typically, they will not invest in a pure idea without it being locked in with comprehensive IP protection.

Visibility – a target on your back

As your business scales, stealth mode will need to be abandoned. You will appear in mass media, your own PR and on public platforms. This new fame can be gratifying and can have many positive benefits for the company.

It also has potentially negative impacts. As you become successful, you call attention to yourself. Bad actors may emerge who want to take advantage of your success.

- "Patent trolls" is the nickname given to companies that acquire patents with the primary intention of blocking other companies and extracting payments.
- Competitors of a comparable level may be jealous of your success and may use their own IP to block your progress.
- Imitators become aware of the attractive market and the problem you are trying to solve. If your success appears to have been achieved easily, they will try to emulate your business either by copying directly or creating a substitute offering.
- Independent inventors who created similar technologies may see an opportunity to accuse you of stealing their ideas or infringing on their patents.

The more successful you are, the more likely that any or all of the above will emerge and create problems for your business. Dealing with these avoidable challenges is an undesirable expense on the business and may distract management attention from the focus on growing the business.

The dark side of disruption

Ever since Clayton Christensen popularised the term "disruptive innovation," it has become a buzz word for high-growth technology companies. In VC pitches, entrepreneurs claim their solution is "disruptive," often without understanding the full strategic implications of the concept.

As your business starts to take off you will come to the attention of larger, incumbent players. When you are a smaller firm, the giants are not interested in you. When you are on track to reaching a billion-dollar scale, you start to make waves in the industry. Your company can no longer be ignored. Indeed, it is quite possible that you will begin to displace the business of some of these larger companies as you gain market share.

The typical action of an incumbent firm will be to disregard the initial threat of a newcomer. As the start-up firm becomes persistent and gains a higher profile in the market, incumbents will take notice but deny that there is a threat. When the new competition is at the scale that the threat is finally acknowledged, the incumbent will then have to take action.

Often that action will be to suppress and extinguish the threat – that is, your company. Often, they will use significant financial or market power. Large incumbents in a technology field will usually have broad patent portfolios and they can bring overwhelming legal firepower into play in ensuring they deliver a "killer" blow to the upstart threatening to disrupt their comfortable industry dominance.

Conclusion

While it is exciting and gratifying to be on the path to becoming a substantial success story, there are significant traps that can ensnare the company on its journey.

Your ability as CEO to navigate these risks, seize opportunities and build intangible value can be the difference between unique sustainable advantage or catastrophic failure.

Chapter 2 – 5 steps to build an IP strategy

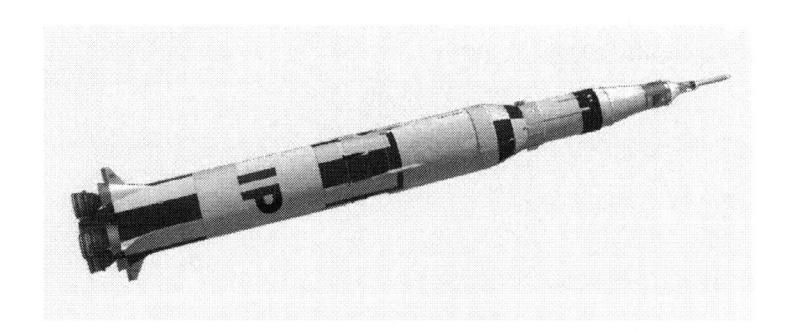

You can build an effective IP strategy by following a 5-step process described in this chapter.

Background

A dramatic shift has occurred in the last 4 decades where intangible value has become a key economic driver for the largest companies and small technology start-ups alike. Despite this evolution, management practices have not kept pace with the changes and gaps have developed.

Growth of intangible value

Ocean Tomo, the intellectual property merchant bank, analysed the components of market value of S&P 500 firms in 1975 and compared those findings against every decade since then. Back in 1975, tangible assets accounted for 83% of enterprise value and intangible assets accounted for 17%. By 1985, the intangible component had grown to 32%. In 1995, the intangible element had grown to 68%, and it reached 80% in 2005. The latest comparable figure for 2020 was 90% intangible value versus 10% tangible value.

After relatively little change in the 200 years since the start of the industrial revolution, the 45 years from 1975 to 2020 have seen a complete inversion in enterprise value from being predominantly tangible (more than 80%) to being predominantly intangible (90%). This has manifested itself in drastic shifts in how companies need to be managed.

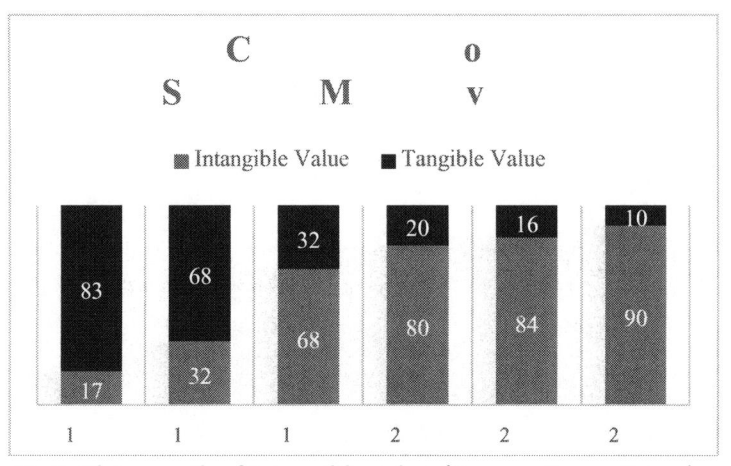

Fig 1: The growth of intangible value *(Source: Ocean Tomo)*

While we can see that intangible value now accounts for 90% of enterprise value for S&P 500 firms, this is not the whole story. In the case of companies such as Pfizer, Facebook or Uber, the intangible portion is significantly higher, and for innovative start-ups with few tangible assets, the intangible component can be close to 100% of enterprise value.

These can be exciting times for companies that can build tremendous value without the need for substantial physical resources. However, a huge threat is lurking beneath this thrilling potential if the intangible value creation is not managed actively.

Value enhancement or value erosion?

For centuries, enterprises faced lower levels of volatility in economic risk. For a farmer or factory owner, swings in land or machinery value could increase or reduce overall asset values by a few percentage points. This made it easy to predict, plan and manage the impact of economic changes.

Today, the stakes are a lot higher for technology companies because of their almost complete dependence on intangible value and its inherent volatility. The "hockey-stick growth" mentioned earlier may increase market value by a factor of 100, while not taking care of its intangible assets can wipe out the company's enterprise value completely.

Popular TV business pitch shows such as "Shark Tank" and "Dragons' Den" have shown the viewing public how the minds of investors work. As mentioned earlier, no matter how exciting an idea is, the investors will always inquire about how it is being protected. Viewers have learned that seasoned investors regard intellectual property as an essential determinant of the investment decision.

The clear implication of this awareness is that all companies are expected to have a well-crafted IP strategy. Thus, it was surprising when research by the UK Intellectual Property Office found that even among large companies, only 22% had a formal IP strategy.

How does IP fall behind?

IP can fall behind when innovators are building their products, markets and business. This is understandable and easily explained.

When innovators are growing their business, they must make decisions about allocation of scarce resources. Survival, development and growth are viewed as the initial priorities. When they are considering short-term priorities, intellectual property protection can be seen as an expensive luxury. The line of thinking is: "I know it will be more expensive to deal with it later. But I will deal with IP when I have more funding/revenue/time."

This is rational business behaviour. However, the obvious and common consequence is that IP ends up being neglected.

As the business evolves, the company will face new challenges with talent, growth, investment and competition. These challenges can be simultaneously daunting and exhilarating. Dealing with intellectual property may be regarded as important but not necessarily urgent, so it still does not receive appropriate attention.

With further levels of success, the gap in IP can become elevated in importance, and sometimes comes to the forefront after an unexpected emergency.

When the company becomes successful, it becomes more visible as a strategic target. It can face attack from competitors and can also appear vulnerable in negotiations with aggressive customers.

A sound IP strategy can put the company in a more confident position when facing these challenges. It can also increase the attractiveness of the company to potential investors.

Indeed, the lack of an IP strategy can expose the intangible value of the company to the risk of being wiped out, as mentioned already.

Intellectual capital enhancement – RACER framework

At IntaVal, we have developed a framework for addressing the almost inevitable gaps in a company's IP strategy.

The 5 steps for implementing and effective IP strategy are:

- Recognition – realising that there are IP gaps and that "something" must be done.
- Audit – reviewing the status quo and establishing a baseline for improvement.
- Concrete action plan – Identifying the steps to be taken to address intangible gaps.
- Execution – mitigating IP risks and building intangible value.
- Review – assessing the effectiveness of the actions against the baseline.

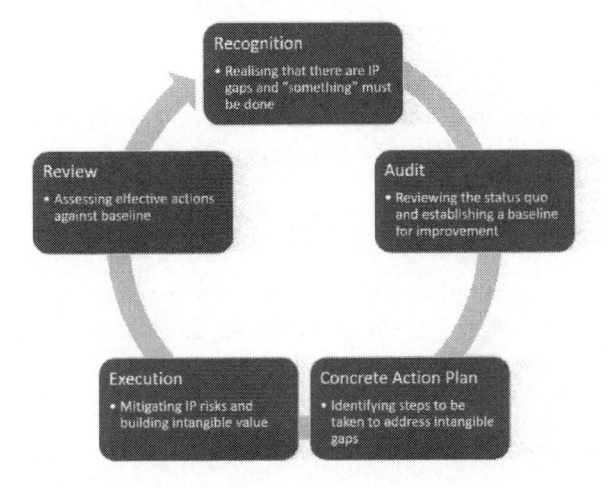

Fig. 2 – RACER Intellectual Capital Enhancement Framework

Recognition

The first step is for management to recognise that there is a potential IP gap and that "something" needs to be done. This may begin in the background as a gnawing concern of management that grows until it cannot be ignored.

Alternatively, the recognition may be in response to external pressure, such as:

- urging by investors to tighten up on IP protection.
- insecurity prior to entering crucial discussions with IP-savvy customers.
- increased competitive activity by rivals.
- accusations by third parties of infringement of their intellectual property.

Audit

A broad intellectual capital audit will cover intangible assets under the headings of human capital (covering competencies and key skills), relational capital (for example customer and supply chain relationships) and structural capital (including trade secrets and formal intellectual property).

The audit follows a structure that examines assets, contracts, ownership, risks and governance. This audit will identify the company's strengths and highlight weaknesses and potential threats. The results of the audit will suggest areas to focus on in a concrete action plan and will also provide a baseline from which to measure improvements.

The content of the audit will vary by company and by industry. According to IP strategist, Donal O'Connell, an IP audit should go beyond merely reviewing IP assets and its scope should encompass at least the following areas:

1	IP awareness & education	7	The IP portfolio of the company
2	IP definition	8	How IP adds value
3	IP maturity & sophistication	9	IP risk
4	IP processes & systems	10	IP resourcing
5	The company's IP position relative to others in its eco system	11	IP in the online world
6	The IP models taken into use	12	IP governance

Source: Donal O'Connell, Chawton Innovation

Concrete action plan

For technology companies, the concrete action plan tends to flow naturally from the audit. Typically, the quickest improvements will be in the areas of trade secret protection and invention discovery leading to patenting activity.

The company will usually have accumulated valuable knowhow and will already follow general disciplines for protection of confidential information. This should be codified in a well-articulated trade secret protection policy.

Trade secrets exist without the need for registration. In law, there are 3 characteristics of trade secrets, namely:

1. they are not generally known;
2. they are of commercial value because they are secret; and,
3. reasonable steps were taken to protect the secrecy.

In Europe for example, to avail of protection under the 2016 European Trade Secrets Directive and other laws, the company will have to maintain evidence of all three characteristics of their trade secrets, namely that the secrets are not generally known, are valuable and that the company took actives steps to protect them.

One step of the concrete action plan is to identify and classify the company's trade secrets. For each of the identified trade secrets, the company must assemble evidence to support the three elements listed above.

In contrast to trade secrets, patents are a means to recognising and protecting valuable inventions via registration.

This is achieved through the following process:

1. invention mining – identifying inventions that the company has created that may be candidates for patent applications.
2. invention disclosure – capturing the details of each invention on a separate invention disclosure form, which becomes a written record that forms the basis for subsequent patent applications.
3. initial patentability search – reviewing each invention to assess its suitability as patentable subject matter, comparing it with the current state of the art and identifying any novel features.
4. patent drafting – if any invention is considered patentable, it will be drafted in a format suitable for submission to the relevant patent office.

5. patent application filing – filing of the patent application with the appropriate national or international patent office.

While this chapter focuses mainly on trade secrets and patents, an effective, comprehensive IP strategy will surround patents and trade secrets with other forms of intellectual property, such as copyrights and trademarks. This will provide a robust, holistic approach to protecting valuable intangible assets.

Execution

After recognition, audit and creation of a concrete action plan, execution should be easy. Right?

Wrong!

Typically, in a fast-growing technology company, the in-house person charged with implementing the concrete action plan will be the CTO. Alternatively, in an inventor-led company, it may be the founder/CEO. When the CTO takes responsibility, the process tends to get derailed by culture. This is because frantic ongoing development continues to pull the CTO away from execution of an IP action plan. If the company has a history of rapid growth without a focus on IP, day-to-day demands will continue to assume a higher priority and IP execution will not be given the required attention.

The solution to this problem is to allocate someone who reports to the CTO as the person with pivotal responsibility. If invention disclosures are being created, that person should have 3 characteristics:

1. the ability to write well,
2. an excellent understanding of the technology and
3. trusted access to the CTO for rapid decisions.

In addition to activities generating patent applications, execution around trade secret protection usually yields pleasant surprises. As the team builds the catalogue of trade secrets, previously invisible intangible assets are identified and made visible, thereby contributing to the accumulation of intangible value.

Review

When a logical RACER process is followed, the review will assess the effectiveness of execution against the baseline established in the audit. The RACER process is an iterative learning environment. As the inventors deal with questions during the patent drafting process, they will find their IP awareness increasing. Active participation in this process will enhance the IP sophistication of everybody involved. This will lead to alertness to further opportunities to reduce IP risks and enhance intangible value.

A one-time process or a cycle?

A project to enhance IP strength often starts out as a one-time process beginning with Recognition and ending with Review, according to the diagram below:

```
Recognition
    ↓
  Audit
    ↓
Concrete Action Plan
    ↓
 Execution
    ↓
  Review
```

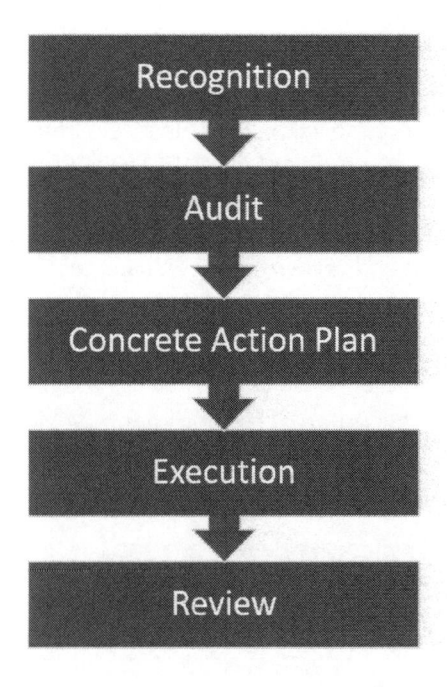

Fig. 3: One-time RACER Process

In a dynamic, innovative company, this linear process will address the IP gaps that initiated the project. Furthermore, during the process, the team will move up the learning curve in understanding intangible value. As they experience the feedback process inherent in invention mining, creating invention disclosures, answering questionnaires and assisting in drafting patent applications, they become more sophisticated in the patenting process. As a result, the quality of subsequent patent applications improves.

The RACER process raises awareness of IP value and alertness to further possibilities. Additionally, if there is a clear increase in enterprise value, there is an economic incentive to repeat the process and extract further value.

So, the one-time RACER (recognition, audit, concrete action plan, execution and review) process leads to a higher awareness of possibilities for further improvement in intangible value. This increased awareness feeds into recognition of other opportunities. That recognition can be the start of a new round of enhancing intangible value, and the one-time RACER process becomes a loop, as in the diagram below.

Fig. 4: Racer Process Cycle

Additional Benefits of a RACER Intangible Value Enhancement Program

The potential return on investment through intangible value enhancement is clear. In addition to developing a process for boosting intangible strength and mitigating potential IP risks, there are potential financial upsides. RACER can be incorporated into a methodology to identify, classify and capitalise intangibles in accordance with existing accounting procedures and existing International Accounting Standards.

Chapter 3 – Intangible value and its components

You got here

The previous chapter showed how intangibles have taken over completely from tangible assets in overall corporate value for technology companies. I could write about how important ideas are for national economies.

But you don't need to be persuaded. You built your business. You have delighted customers. Now you have bigger ambitions. Furthermore, you know that IP is important. That's why you are here.

That is the "Recognition" part of the RACER framework.

You have identified that there are gaps in your IP strategy. You may or may not have performed a formal IP audit.

That brings us to "Concrete Actions" and "Execution" in the RACER framework. Now let's do something about it.

IP cheat sheet

IP people are passionate.

Every day there are examples of blatant misunderstanding about the different types of IP. This triggers our passionate reflexes.

We always want to shout at the radio when the business correspondent (who should know better) comes on and says something like "Company X has been sued for copyright infringement. Apparently, they were not able to patent their trademark on time."

In truth, the IP community is at fault for expecting business decision makers to understand IP. Often the IP department resides in its own silo and expects the corporate strategy to fit in with the IP strategy. IP conferences constantly have themes that insist that companies should create posts such as Chief IP Officer (CIPO) and that the CIPO should have a seat on the company's board. People espousing these themes (invariably members of a beleaguered IP department) are emboldened by the relative growth in intangible value mentioned in intangible value mentioned in Chapter 2 to support their assertion that "IP's time has finally come."

A more enlightened approach is for the IP department to start with corporate strategy in mind and craft an IP strategy that can be explained in terms of the overall business strategy.

In this book, I want to make the business leader come close to becoming an "innovation Ninja" and become able to make knowledgeable decisions about the company's IP strategy and direction.

Before we launch into any detail, let's just make sure you can distinguish between the main types of intellectual property.

They are summarised in this table and explained in more detail in the table that follows.

IP type	Subject matter	Registration Method	Lifetime
Patent	Inventions, machines, processes. Excludes abstract ideas and algorithms.	Registration with relevant patent office.	20 years
Trademarks	Brands, symbols, logos, sounds, colours, shapes	Registration with relevant trademark office.	Unlimited, subject to registration
Copyright	Artistic creations, music, images, movies, software	No registration in Europe. Automatic, when committed to tangible form	Lifetime of author plus 50-100 years, depending on the country's laws.
Trade secret	Anything of value, kept intentionally secret, that confers competitive advantage.	No registration	Unlimited, for the lifetime of the secret

Fig 5: IP Cheat Sheet

It is worth learning about the distinctions between these different areas.

Patents

A patent usually covers a novel invention, machine or process.

A patent is a right granted to an inventor to exclude someone else from importing, making, using, selling or offering to sell the invention.

A patent is a right that is granted through registration with the relevant patent office, which can be national (such as the USPTO in the USA or the JPO in Japan) or regional (such as the European Patent Office). The lifetime of a patent is typically 20 years from the date of filing, provided the regular maintenance fees are paid in each relevant national patent office.

Trademarks / Service Marks

A trademark may be a brand name, symbol, word, logo or other identification of a product or service that indicates its origin and distinguishes it from a product or service made or offered by others.

Trademarks are covered by the Paris Convention (1883) and relevant national laws. This means that if an application is filed in one contracting state an application may be filed in another contracting state within 6 months and enjoy protection from the date of the original home-state application.

Trademarks are registered according to the class of product or service. Under the Nice Classification of Goods and Services, goods come under classes 1 to 34 and services come under classes 35 to 45.

For example, Class 7 covers products such as machines and machine tools. Within each class, there are sub-classes. Pneumatic door openers are classed as 070520. Pneumatic door closers are 070552.

One trademark may cover several classes. For example, a high-end fashion brand may be registered for jewellery (class 14), leather luggage (class 18) and clothing & shoes (class 25).

Costs of registration and maintenance are based per class, per country. For a small company, registrations in several classes in multiple countries can be an expensive exercise, so the investment should be focused on what makes the most sense for the business.

Copyright

Copyright applies to original creative works such as art, drama, visual images or software. Under the Berne Convention for the Protection of Literary and Artistic Works (1886), more commonly known as the "Berne Convention," authors can expect the same treatment in foreign contracting states as if they were nationals of that state.

Unlike patents and trademarks, copyrights do not require registration. Once an original creative work is committed in tangible form it enjoys copyright protection from that time. A musical idea, for example, will not be protected until it is written down or recorded.

While registration is not a requirement, in jurisdictions where registration is provided for under national law (such as in the USA), a registered copyright will provide *prima facie* evidence of the ownership of copyright in infringement cases and allow the owner claim statutory damages and attorney fees.

While the copyright symbol © can be applied to copyrighted material, it is not necessary to affix it in order to enjoy protection. The only reason to use it these days is to ensure infringers do not benefit from reduced damages where they could claim "innocent infringement" of the copyright.

The lifetime of a copyright depends on how it is specified in national legislation and this period has changed as legislation has been amended over the years. Nowadays, the typical life is somewhere between 50 to 100 years after the death of the author or the first public performance. In most jurisdictions, the copyright will pass into the public domain 70 years after the death of the author.

Trade secrets

Trade secrets are not discussed much in legal and intellectual property circles because they cannot be registered as formal IP rights. However, they are gaining in profile because of recent developments in legislation in important global jurisdictions, and because they are featuring in high-profile litigation.

Large parts of intangible value in fast-growing technology companies fall under the category of trade secrets, so any integrated IP strategy must pay close attention to the importance of trade secrets.

IP strategy covered in this book

While there are other types of IP with relevance in specific areas, this book will focus on the three areas that are most relevant to technology companies – patents, trademarks, and trade secrets.

Copyright is no doubt important to some companies, but I have chosen to exclude a detailed discussion of it from this book in order to focus on the other areas of common interest to growth-stage technology companies.

Do you need to protect IP?

Unusually for a book on IP, this book does not state you *must* register intellectual property at every opportunity. Because the focus is on IP strategy, registration decisions should always be made in conjunction with the overall corporate strategy.

It comes down to two questions:

- Is this IP directly linked to a competitive advantage?
- Does the product or service have the market potential to justify the investment of time, effort and money into filing for protection?

A further consideration relates to the appetite and capability to enforce those rights. Even when intellectual property protections are in place, a company may not be able to identify infringements or have the legal and financial capacity to enforce its rights.

As you will see in the chapters on patents and trade secrets, there may also be tension between different types of protection where it may make sense to not file for a patent where trade secret protection would be more effective.

Intellectual Capital

Intangible value is not just based on formal IP. Intellectual capital can be analysed under 3 headings:

- Human Capital is where all intangible value creation springs from. All new business opportunities begin in the heads of your team members. This can manifest itself in areas such as knowhow, teamwork capability, skills, experience and employee adaptability.
- Relational Capital is where the value of the business can be experienced. It arises from relationships with customers, the supply chain and investors. It manifests itself in customer loyalty, customer satisfaction and, ultimately, sustainable revenue.
- Structural Capital is where intangible value is systematised. It can be in culture, systems and processes. It can be protected in the forms of IP we have already mentioned – formal IP such as patents, trademarks and copyright – or as trade secrets and other forms of protection.

While structural capital is the primary focus of this book, the broader spectrum of intellectual capital will be examined more in the final section of this book.

Chapter 4 – Patents

A patent is a form of intellectual property that gives the owner the right to exclude others from importing, making, using or selling an invention for a limited period. In return for this protection, the inventor must make a public disclosure of the invention.

Different types of patents

In the USA, there are 3 main types of patent – utility, design and plant patents.

Utility patents

Utility patents protect what is typically considered an "invention." There are three requirements for a patent to be granted: it must be useful, novel and non-obvious. Each of these requirements will be discussed in more detail below.

Patents have a typical maximum lifetime of 20 years from filing. This is considered long enough for the inventor to build a customer base and market reputation before others are allowed to use the invention without permission from the inventor.

A sub-category of utility patents is the business model patent. One famous example is Amazon's one-click purchasing feature. Between the increased revenue the feature brought to Amazon's website and its royalties that it received from licensing to companies such as Apple, this patent was estimated to be worth $2.4 billion to Amazon annually until its expiry in 2017.

Business method patents proliferated since the decision in the *State Street Bank and Trust Company v. Signature Financial Group, Inc.* case in 1998, but have faced huge uncertainty since the 2014 *Alice Corporation v. CLS Bank* case, where they invalidated a business-method patent based on an abstract idea. In the intervening 5 years, there was considerable pessimism around the prospects for software patents. However, in March 2019, Andrei Iancu, the Director of the USPTO said in a speech that the US Supreme Court "never said that all automation with computers is per se ineligible."

Tip: you can really focus the minds of your patent people by asking them about software-related patents: "Yes, but how does it pass the Alice test?"

Design patents

A design patent protects the unique features of a product's shape, outline or colour. The design is an ornamental feature that does not have practical utility. For example, a bottle shape design could be protected because of its ornamental qualities but the design of the screw thread on the bottle cap cannot because of its functionality. The lifetime of a design patent is 17 years.

Design patents should not be considered inferior to utility patents. In their billion-dollar case against Samsung, Apple asserted several utility and design patents including one that that described the iPhone and iPad as having "on-screen icons" and another one describing the design as "a thin rectangular cuboid with rounded corners."

Plant patents

It is possible to patent plant varieties that are propagated via asexual reproduction (i.e., not by planting seeds). Plant patents represent a small proportion of total patents but can be very important for organisations working in the area of plant genetics. Some examples would be a new variety of tomato with a sharper taste or flowers that are resistant to specific diseases.

Non-USA patent types

We described 3 main types of patent in the American system. In other parts of the world, the same division of utility and design patent are not used. Indeed, designs themselves are not normally protected by patent, even though several countries offer other ways of protecting designs. The US term "utility patents" is normally described internationally as "industrial patents" or simply "patents".

To make matters more confusing, some countries, in addition to offering industrial patents, also offer the option of a "utility model patent," which is not the same as the US "utility patent." This is an alternative that has a lower standard of examination, cheaper filing fees and a shorter life (7 years instead of 20 years). However, because the patent application does not have to undergo strict examination, it may not be as robust if it is ever relied upon in patent litigation. This option can be attractive to small companies that want a less expensive way to get protection and who do not intend to use it in court against potential adversaries.

Only a few countries offer the option of the utility model patent, the most notable being China and Germany.

Patentable subject matter

Even if an invention is novel and inventive, it may not be eligible for patenting if it is not considered patentable subject matter. The rules vary from jurisdiction to jurisdiction.

For example, most jurisdictions exclude mathematical theorems, abstract concepts and algorithms from patentability. Most people understand that to mean that software is not patentable, but there are exceptions according to jurisdiction.

USA eligibility

In the USA, patent eligibility is covered by Section 101, Title 35 U.S.C. which state you may be able to patent "any new and useful process, machine, manufacture or composition of matter, or any new and useful improvement thereof."

The 1998 **State Street Bank v. Signature Financial Group** case was a landmark decision that supported the concept of business processes being patentable. In its decision, the court found that a financial product such as a share price calculation could be patentable as a "useful, concrete and tangible result." This concept was further supported by the interim guidelines issued by the USPTO in October 2005.

As a result of this supportive environment for business methods, software patents rose from 20% of all US patents in 1991 to around 50% by 2011.

Over the years, questions were raised by those who disagreed with the *State Street* decision, and in the case *In re Bilski* (2008) the Federal Circuit overturned the "useful, concrete and tangible result" (UCTR) test. This decision was further affirmed by the Supreme court in ***Bilski v. Kappos*** (2010).

Software patent eligibility was dealt further blows by ***Mayo v. Prometheus*** (2012) and ***Alice v. CLS Bank*** (2014) with the introduction of a 2-step test. In the 2-step test, the examiner must first determine if the invention is directed towards an abstract idea or natural principle. If it is, the second step is to ascertain if it is implemented in an inventive manner or merely solved through a conventional approach.

The *Alice* case concluded that a simple generic computer implementation of an abstract idea is patent ineligible. It is not an exaggeration to say that this single decision sent shock waves through the patent community that are felt to this day.

It changed the balance of power in the technology community. This reversal of the ease of patenting abstract models gave a potent tool for accused infringers to fight back against patent owners. This new position led to 90% of disputed software enabled business method patents being invalidated by the Court of Appeals for the Federal Circuit in 2015.

Patent eligibility in Europe

In Europe, the patent system is governed by the European Patent Convention. The guidance in EPC Article 52 states that patents can be granted for inventions that "are new, involve an inventive step and are susceptible of industrial application." However, it is silent on the positive question of what exactly is allowed. It simply refers to a non-exhaustive list of excluded subject matter, namely:

- discoveries, scientific theories and mathematical methods;
- aesthetic creations;
- schemes, rules and methods for performing mental acts, playing games or doing business, and programs for computers;
- presentations of information.

EPC Article 53 goes on to list categories that will not receive patents:

- inventions the commercial exploitation of which would be contrary to "public order" or morality;
- plant or animal varieties or essentially biological processes for the production of plants or animals;
- methods for treatment of the human or animal body by surgery or therapy and diagnostic methods practised on the human or animal body.

Requirements of a patent

As mentioned, the 3 requirements for a patent are that it must be useful, novel and non-obvious. While you don't need to have an in-depth understanding of the patent examination process, a general overview is useful to guide your decisions about preparing and filing applications.

The trade-off – protection for publication

As noted at the start of this chapter, patent protection is given in exchange for publication of the patented information. Publication serves the purpose of letting the world know exactly what has been protected. It serves the greater purpose of letting the world benefit from the ingenuity of the invention, even though no one else can practise it during the life of the patent without the permission of the inventor.

Once the patent expires, is abandoned or is invalidated, everybody is free to use it. This is how generic drug manufacturers can offer lower-priced alternatives after a rival drug has gone "off patent."

For some inventors, the obligation to publish may be a deterrent to patenting. As soon as their patent is published, it becomes visible to the world. This publication could be a "roadmap" for rivals to "invent around" the patent and thereby bypass the protections. Furthermore, companies that take a long-term view may not like the idea that the patent has a limited life. Therefore, some companies choose to protect their inventions as trade secrets rather than patenting them. We will explore trade secrets in later chapters.

Application process

For an established company with a suite of technologies, it is theoretically possible to do most of the work yourself or use a low-cost online service to file a patent. However, this is difficult and is less likely to result in a patent being granted. Furthermore, when it comes to relying on such patents in subsequent conflict, these do-it-yourself patents are rarely robust enough to withstand vigorous litigation.

If the company has the financial resources, it is strongly recommended to use a professional firm that can provide more robust outcomes and probably save money in the long term.

The typical patent application process is:

1) Identify an invention;
2) Write down the details;
3) Perform preliminary searches;
4) Refine application through redrafting;
5) File application.

Patent office examination

Before considering how to prepare a patent application, it is useful to understand how the patent office deals with patent applications.

While there are variations by patent office, the United States Patent and Trademark Office (USPTO) is used for this illustration. In the USA, you can file a non-provisional patent application immediately or you can start with a provisional application.

When a non-provisional patent application is filed at the USPTO and the filing fee paid (currently US$720 for large entities), the filing date is recorded and a serial number is assigned to the file at the patent office.

Provisional applications on the other hand, are given a filing date but will not be examined until they are converted into a non-provisional application. At that stage, it will be assigned a new serial number and will be given the same priority date as the original provisional application filing date. If a non-provisional application is not lodged within 12 months, the provisional application will lapse.

Office actions

Non-provisional applications are picked up by patent examiners on a first-filed-first-served basis. The examiners normally respond within 1-3 years with their assessment as to whether the application is novel and non-obvious. This written response is called an "office action."

Many inventors abandon their application when they receive an office action saying that their application is obvious or not novel. It is a mistake to give up without investigating more.

As an inventor, you should not be discouraged if you receive a negative decision from the USPTO. Most patent applications receive such an office action. You can treat it as an opportunity to work with your patent attorney to draft a response to narrow the claims to get around the prior art that was found.

In making your decision to respond, you should be guided by 2 factors:

1. The strength of the patent examiner's arguments
2. The attractiveness of your product – the market may have changed since you filed your original application.

Expediting the process

While the first office action will normally come within 1-3 years, you have the option of paying a premium to have your application examined in a fast-track process. Under this process, you can expect to receive the office action within 4-6 months.

Furthermore, if one of the inventors is aged over 65 years, the fee for the expedited examination can be waived.

Patent pending

After a patent application has been filed, the inventor is permitted to designate the related product as "Patent Pending." However, such designation has very little immediate legal impact because the patent cannot be enforced before it has been granted.

The "Patent Pending" marking can be used to warn potential infringers that an application is in process and that if it is granted, the inventor may be able to seek an injunction, seizure or damages (sometimes back-dated to the time of the first application).

This in itself can serve as a useful protection and disincentive to bad behaviour by competitors.

Chapter 5 – Invention mining and the patenting process

Invention mining

Invention mining is the process of finding inventions within an organisation that could be candidates for subsequent inclusion in a patent application process.

Invention mining should not be confused with "patent mining," which is the process of assessing a portfolio of existing issued patents and patent applications to identify assets that can be used for licensing, trading, divestiture or other activities.

Invention mining can take various forms depending on the maturity of the ideas to be mined.

- Identifying existing inventions that were created internally in the past.
- Encouraging employees to take their ongoing research findings or other ideas and form them into potential inventions.
- Invention sessions where people from different disciplines or departments come together to perform joint invention activities. Often these unusual combinations of approach can lead to novel and inventive ideas.
- Futurecasting, where employees envision future challenges and formulate solutions to build a pipeline of future-oriented patents.

The ideas can be captured by self-directed teams using an invention disclosure form, or the sessions could operate under the guidance of an experienced facilitator.

Potential barriers to invention mining

Clearly the process of invention does not follow a simple formula. Some of the barriers to invention mining are:

- Secrecy – researchers and inventors are, by nature, secretive and protective of their creative "babies." Discussing their ideas outside a tight circle can be uncomfortable for them. They may even be hesitant about sharing with their colleagues within the broader organisation.
- "I'm not Edison" – the mystique around invention often leads people to think that their own ideas do not measure up to the standard that could be viewed as a valid, patentable invention. The first step of brainstorming is to encourage as many ideas as possible without judgement or censorship. Criticism (or even self-criticism) stifles the creativity and can impede the flow of ideas. Filtering should be reserved until later stages of the process.
- "Nothing new under the sun" – this is a variant of "I'm not Edison" that implies that all the best innovation has already been created and it is impossible to come up with new, valuable inventions. The actual quote is biblical. It appears in Ecclesiastes 1:9 in the words of Solomon:
  "What has been will be again, what has been done will be done again; there is nothing new under the sun."
  To rebut that, consider that the 10 millionth US patent was granted in June 2018. If you average that over the 228 years since the first US patent was

issued in 1790, you would expect the 9 millionth patent to have issued as far back as 1995. Actually, the 9 millionth patent was issued in 2015. With one million patents issued in just three years, it is clear that the rate of patent filing activity is increasing in recent years.
- Academic approach – this is a double-edged sword. Researchers continuously look for something new. Academic researchers are excellent at documenting their findings. Furthermore, through literature review, they are very good at identifying key areas of prior art, which is very useful in aiding the patent drafting process.

  One drawback of academic research is that publication credibility is supported by showing how similar the research findings are to the results of other respected researchers. That instinct can hamper the important element of demonstrating an "inventive step" in making differentiated inventions that will increase the prospect of the patent application being successful.

  Furthermore, the pressure to disclose academic research findings publicly can introduce self-generated prior art that would jeopardise the possibility of filing patents.
- Budgetary constraints – depending on the company's budget, the cost of patent applications could be a disincentive to file multiple patent applications. This can be exacerbated by the anticipation of an even higher level of patent filing and maintenance fees for

protection in multiple jurisdictions over the lifetime of the patent.

- Disclosure reluctance – a requirement of patent protection is that the invention will need to be disclosed and published for the world to see. As discussed in Chapter 4, it may be more desirable to keep the idea as a trade secret, rather than disclose the invention in the patent application. However, because the first step of invention mining is to merely gather candidates for patenting, this disclosure reluctance should not be allowed to limit the flow of possibilities. The decision to disclose via patent filing or not will come later when the disclosures are all reviewed by the company's invention review board (more about that later).
- Philosophical opposition to patenting – in some technological circles, there is antipathy towards patents in general. Some people believe that "ideas should be free" and that patent protection prevents the free exchange of ideas and thereby inhibits broader innovation. This can foster an anti-patent and anti-IP culture that can be difficult to overcome.
- Enforcement difficulties – obtaining a patent is one challenge but some people argue that it is not worth having patents if you are not able to enforce them. Some companies may not have the appetite to enforce their rights when they suspect infringement and may also be deterred by the potential costs of enforcement activities, full-blown litigation that may exceed budgets and with uncertainty regarding the probability of success.

Invention harvesting

A typical process for invention harvesting will be:

1) Collection of invention disclosures.
2) Inventor interviews to add depth to the information on the invention disclosure form.
3) Patentability review and search.
4) Drafting of the patent application.
5) Separate attorney review.
6) Submission of application to the patent office.

Large organisations may have their own internal patent attorneys, which gives them the choice of how much work to perform internally and how much to outsource. Companies without those resources will outsource steps 2) to 6).

Because of the cost involved in each step, the company may undertake reviews between stages. Usually there will be a review between step 1) and step 2) to select which disclosures to prioritise for outsourcing work.

In setting the budget for outsourcing, it is common to group steps 2) and 3) together and agree a separate fee for steps 4) and 5). This is because it is common for ideas to fail during patentability review and search, so there is no point continuing to incur costs on that disclosure.

Step 6) involves filing the patent application with the relevant patent office and paying a fixed fee.

Invention review board

The purpose of invention mining is to build an inventory of the inventions that already exist within a company. As a matter of good governance, an invention review board (IRB) should be convened regularly to review new invention disclosures and make decisions whether or not to progress each disclosure through as a patent application.

The IRB should be composed of members who are qualified to make such decisions. The board should be large enough to cover the business objectives but not so large as to make its operation unwieldy. The members can include the CTO (who is intimately familiar with the subject matter), general counsel (for legal implications), and a representative of marketing (to decide if the invention has commercial merit) and other relevant management team members.

In an innovative company, it is important for the IRB to meet frequently enough to be able to capture the rapid flow of new inventions. Another reason for the IRB to meet frequently is to facilitate feedback to the inventors. If too much time elapses between the submission of the invention disclosure and the IRB feedback, inventors may lose motivation to report new inventions.

Chapter 6 – How patents are enforced

Chapter 4 outlined what a patent is and how to obtain patent protection. However, the word "protection" might be misleading.

A granted patent does not automatically prevent people from copying your idea. Patent infringement is not a criminal offence, so it is not enforced by the police.

It is the responsibility of the patent owner to identify any potential infringements and take legal action in court to protect the company's rights. In other words, you have to assert your rights.

Defences against accusations of infringement

What happens when you assert your rights against a suspected infringer?

The two most common grounds for defence against an accusation of infringement are non-infringement and invalidity.

A defendant can claim non-infringement by outlining how the product in question is different in some material way from the exact wording of the claim in the patent. If this can be proven, the defendant can escape the accusation of patent infringement.

The second way a defendant can win is by proving the patent is in some way invalid. The defendant will search for evidence to prove that there is a flaw in the patent that renders the entire patent invalid or at least the relevant claims that are being asserted. This can be done in many ways. For example, the defendant might find some piece of published prior art that was not disclosed or discovered by the original patent examiner. This would cause the patent to be revoked on grounds of lack of novelty. They might query the validity of the patent on the grounds that the invention was not patentable subject matter. They might rely on expert testimony that the invention would have been obvious to "a person normally skilled in the art" at the time that the patent application was filed and thus did not have the required inventive step.

In the end, a court will decide that the patent is:

1) Valid and infringed;
2) Valid but not infringed;
3) Invalid and not infringed; or,
4) Invalid and infringed

For the plaintiff to prevail, the patent must be found both valid and infringed. In all four cases apart from the first one above, both conditions are not satisfied simultaneously, and the defendant will escape.

What does this mean for patent owners?

When you suspect your patent is being infringed, you must first gather data and ascertain the facts. A finding of infringement is rarely a black-and-white situation. American patent cases are heard in courts in front of a jury.

Because the jury members are not required to have legal or technical expertise, there is a process to assist their deliberations. A key part of the trial will be when the judge takes the relevant claims of the patent and translates it for the jury. The judge will break down the language of the claim, phrase by phrase and translate it into a glossary for the jury. The jury will then apply each sub-phrase of the patent claim to see if it matches the accused product. If every element matches, infringement will be found.

As a patent owner, before you accuse someone of infringement, your preparation may follow a similar process. It is not enough to merely suspect infringement. You will have to identify products that are suspected of infringing and produce evidence of use (EOU) by the infringer.

The document that maps each element of the patent claim to the accused product is called a "claim chart." This process requires a lot of commitment as the legal and engineering costs of preparing this documentation can run to tens of thousands of dollars per patent.

The second defence to a patent infringement action is invalidity. The implication for the patent owner is that any accusation can invite an attack on the patent itself. If the patent or key claims are invalidated, it could destroy the underlying asset. That is why patent owners need to give careful consideration before launching any accusations that could ultimately lead to the loss of key assets.

Indeed, accused infringers have in recent years used the threat of invalidation proceedings successfully as a potent tool to resist licensing discussions. In the USA, the cost to request a re-examination of a patent is far cheaper than a long-drawn-out litigation, so there is an incentive for accused infringers to respond by attacking the patent.

If their challenge is successful, the patent will be invalidated, resulting in huge damage for the owner of the patent. If the patent is invalidated in a dispute with one party, the same patent will be no longer available to generate licensing revenues from other licensees.

The fear that a valuable patent could be invalidated can serve as a deterrent to the owner from exercising his rights against a suspected infringer who has the ability to launch such a counterattack.

Assertion licensing

The owner of valuable intellectual property has the right to exclude others from using that IP. This allows the owner to carve out an exclusive market or charge a premium for products.

Another way to profit from intellectual property is to allow others to use the invention or use the brand by paying a license fee to benefit from access to those rights.

Assertion licensing is when the owner of important intellectual property – usually patents or trademarks – identifies people operating in the market who are believed to be infringing the IP and requires them to sign up as licensees to pay a fee for enjoying that benefit.

The elements of an assertion licensing program include:

- Portfolio analysis – reviewing your own portfolio of IP to identify patents that could be licensed. This analysis will review patents under classifications such

as patent strength, relevance to a technology market and identifiability of potential infringement.
- Market investigation – for a patent that is suspected of being infringed broadly, the market investigation will involve identifying potential infringers and estimating the scale of their infringement. Large market player infringement may be obvious, even without investigation. For smaller infringers, it may be necessary to do internet searches, interview competitors, attend trade shows, and buy suspected infringing product.
- Building a case – for suspected cases of infringement, it is good practice to build claim charts and evidence of use. Claim charts are prepared by engineers and attorneys who are specialised in looking at a product's features and mapping the features of the accused product to each phrase of a patent's claims. This is a very specialised and expensive activity to perform. If the product does not match each phrase of one complete claim in a patent, it does not infringe the claim.
- Approach – when the evidence is collected, you can approach the alleged infringer and notify them that you suspect their product of infringement. This must be done with precise legal detail, because if your approach could be accused of being frivolous or a groundless threat, the other side may be able to take a counter action against you. Furthermore, as mentioned already, you also face the risk of having your patent invalidated.

- Negotiation and settlement – in situations where the accused infringer accepts that you have a case and that your IP is valuable for their business, they may engage in a discussion that leads ultimately to a settlement that covers compensation for past infringement and a payment for peaceful future use of the IP.
- Litigation – if the accused infringer refuses to engage, or if the expected price positions are too far apart, it may be necessary to request the courts to make a determination about what is the fairest solution. Many companies find IP litigation undesirable because it can take several years, with the associated costs, uncertainty and hostile relationships that will develop between the parties.

Assertion license royalty calculation

If the licensing activity leads to litigation, some infringers will look on the calculation of the costs of settlement via license agreement versus the probability of winning at each stage of the case. Assuming a license based on that probability, the maximum average exposure would be:

Litigation payout x Probability of losing x Probability of action being taken x Probability of being identified.

So, as an example, a large player in a remote country among several other players might apply the following logic:

- **Potential litigation payout:** $100 million.
- **Probability of losing:** 60%.

- **Probability of an action being taken against this player:** 10%.
- **Probability of infringement being identified:** 10%.

In that case, the risk-weighted exposure is:

$$\$100,000,000 \times 60\% \times 10\% \times 10\% = \$600,000$$

After that, the question comes down to the appetite for risk on both sides, the anticipated legal costs for both parties and the attitude to the impact of a long process on both parties.

Often the licensing decision will come down to taking a view of the cost of the license compared with the litigation-avoidance calculation of the net risk-weighted exposure.

For a licensor, the mathematics can be changed if they reduce their risk in each element through more thorough investigations to identify infringement, an aggressive attitude towards asserting their rights and detailed legal preparations.

Chapter 7 – Patent strategies

You will recall from Chapter 4 that a patent is a right to exclude. It is important to understand that it is not a right to use an invention.

Even if you have a patent, you might not be allowed to use it if it infringes upon someone else's patent. For example, if a product A-B has patented features (A and B) and you invent an improvement (C), you cannot make a product A-B-C without permission from the owner of the patent that covers A and B. Similarly, that owner can make product A-B but cannot make the improved A-B-C product without your permission.

To be very clear: just because you have a patent, don't think you are not infringing on other patents. In a crowded technological field, other people may have overlapping patents in the same area. IP strategy concerns building an awareness of the competitive landscape and crafting strategies to address potential risks.

Patent prosecution strategies

While this book is about building IP strategy, it does not suggest that every invention should be patented. All decisions about protecting intellectual property should be driven by the extent to which the assets will support the overall corporate strategy.

In a criminal context, "prosecution" involves charging someone with a crim and then putting them on trial. "Prosecution" in the patent world refers to the interaction between the inventor, representatives and the patent offices to draft, file and manage the progress of a patent application.

Patent prosecution is complicated. It is possible to do elements on a do-it-yourself basis. However, if you want to create a portfolio of reliable intangible assets, it is advisable to engage a professional practitioner to advise on patent prosecution strategies and manage the execution.

Patent protection is geographical

Patent protection is afforded in individual jurisdictions by applying to national patent offices or a regional office such as the European Patent Office. Enforcement is also on a country-by-country basis.

Furthermore, the purpose of a patent is not just to protect an invention from being made by someone else. You will recall that if you have a patent, you can prevent someone from making, using, selling, offering to sell or importing products that are covered by the patent. It may be that the patents refer to products that have different levels of relationships with different geographical markets.

This means that when you are considering territories to register your patent, you should give thought to where something is made, used, sold, offered for sale or imported as possible places to seek protection.

For example, one product may be manufactured locally for the local market. In that case, it would make sense to just file for a patent in that territory.

Conversely, a German manufacturer could make a product for its home market and may have ambitions to sell it in the USA in future. That company could also have a direct competitor based in France who has their products manufactured in China. In that case, they should consider registering the patent in Germany, France, China and the USA.

Patent filing choices

For fast-growing technology companies, there may be strategic imperatives to file a patent application quickly. The USA used to take a first-to-invent approach to patent ownership but now it follows a first-to-file approach in harmony with most global patent systems. Because of this, a speedy first filing may be necessary if a technology company wants to establish its primary position with a novel technology before any competitors can join the fray.

As mentioned earlier, countries such as Germany and China offer the option of filing an application for a Utility Model Patent. This is a patent application that has a lower level of scrutiny, can be granted more rapidly and enjoys lower filing fees. If you want to obtain rapid protection, one strategic approach is to apply for a utility model patent and file a full patent application simultaneously. Then you can seek to abandon the Utility Model patent when the full patent is granted ultimately.

If the preference is to file the first application in the USA, there is the option of filing a provisional patent application initially instead of a full patent application.

When a provisional application is filed in the USPTO, the filing date is recorded, an application number is attached. However, there is no further action taken, and the patent application will not be examined until a further non-provisional application is filed. The patent application will include a detailed description, drawings and at least one claim, usually a "dummy claim" that is inserted as a place holder.

Then the inventor has up to 12 months to file a further application with the full details of patent claims to convert the provisional into a non-provisional application. When the final patent is granted, it will enjoy the benefit of the original filing date as the priority date of the patent.

When an inventor is refining the technology, there is a temptation to wait until it is perfect before filing the patent application. In the first-to-file environment, delays of even one day can mean that a rival inventor may file an application that could predate your application and become the prior art that defeats your application. In fast-moving environments, it is advisable to file provisional applications quickly. Indeed, if more features and variations are developed, you can file more provisional applications within the 12-month window and combine them into one non-provisional application in the conversion stage.

The advantages of the provisional application:

- It is quicker to prepare the application because you do not need to specify the claims in detail.
- You do not need to go to the expense of searching for prior art before lodging the application.
- The initial filing fees are lower.

- The rapid filing allows you to get an earlier priority date for your invention rather than wait for searches and the time involved in drafting a full application.
- You have 12 more months to test the market before deciding to move ahead with the expense and effort of a full patent application.
- If you decide to abandon the application within the first 12 months, it will never reach the 18-month marker where the application is published, so your competitors will not see the details of your invention.

The provisional filing route has more advantages than disadvantages, but you should note the following:

- While the initial filing fee is lower, you will have to pay the full filing fee when you ultimately convert into a non-provisional application within the first 12 months. The total fees will be more expensive than if you had filed the non-provisional application from the start.
- Because the drafting is not as demanding as for a non-provisional application, there can be a temptation to not use an attorney to draft the provisional application. While this is possible, it may become problematic if poor drafting limits your options subsequently when you prepare the non-provisional application.
- Because you do not have to perform searches regarding novelty and inventive step, when you perform searches some months later as part of your conversion, you may come across troublesome prior

art that should have warned you earlier in the process.

"Global" applications

It is common to hear that somebody has a "global patent" or a "global application." There is no such thing as a global patent. It is a system of jurisdiction-by-jurisdiction registration. Similarly, enforcement is typically jurisdiction by jurisdiction.

If you wish to register your patent internationally, you have three options:

1. Simultaneous direct filing – for countries not parties to the Paris Convention, you need to file your application in each national office. Note: this is almost irrelevant to tech companies because practically every country of interest is a party to the Paris Convention – 177 members including all major international economies.
2. Paris Convention filing – if the original patent application is filed in a country that is party to the Paris Convention, applications can be filed in other countries within 12 months of the original filing and enjoy the benefit of the priority date of the original filing.
3. PCT filing – this is an international patent filing mechanism that is very popular among fast-growing tech companies with global ambitions. We describe it in more detail below.

Patent Cooperation Treaty (PCT)

The Patent Cooperation Treaty (PCT) is an international mechanism between contracting jurisdictions to streamline the international application process for patents. There are 152 contracting states, covering all major economies that are relevant for high-growth tech companies.

If the patent application is filed in one contracting jurisdiction, the inventor has the option within 12 months to designate the application as an international application under the PCT. This sets a process in train for the patent office to notify the World Intellectual Property Organisation (WIPO) in Geneva, Switzerland, and request an international search report (ISR) simultaneously. At 16 months, the international search report and non-binding written opinion are issued. The application is published internationally 18 months after the original filing date. All of this comes under the "International Phase" of the patent application.

Under the PCT process, the "National Phase" comes into effect 12 months after publication (that is, 30 months after the initial filing). At this stage, you must nominate the individual national patent offices where you need protection. When your application enters the National Phase, you will start to incur translation costs, national filing fees and national patent attorney fees. However, as an incentive to encourage inventors to follow the PCT route, many national patent offices have adopted a policy of considering some of the work already performed and offer reduced filing fees for entering into the national phase.

Month	Activity	Phase
0	File local application	Local filing
12	File PCT application	International phase
16	Receive ISR and written opinion	International phase
18	International publication of application	International phase
30	Enter national phase	National phase

Fig 6: PCT Timeline

Which route is preferable?

Of the three routes to international filing mentioned earlier – direct route, Paris Convention and PCT – we have already mentioned that the direct route is least popular when filing in multiple jurisdictions because most countries of interest are parties to both the Paris Convention and the PCT. So, that leaves Paris Convention and PCT as the main choices.

Most companies prefer PCT for a few reasons:

- Under the Paris Convention, national filing must be made with 12 months of the original local filing. The

30 months allowed by the PCT gives the company more time to establish the technology and decide which jurisdictions will require protection and justify the cost.
- If the filing is made under the PCT, the translation costs, filing fees and local patent attorney fees will not become due until 30 months after the original filing date. This gives a cash-flow advantage over the Paris Convention, where the costs will be incurred after just 12 months.
- If the search report and written opinion find that the invention is not patentable, the application can be abandoned before multiple international filing costs are incurred.
- While there are some additional administration fees in connection with the PCT application, some national patent offices offer discounted filing fees at the National Phase, which usually means a lower overall cost.

Comment

The foregoing section misses out on one aspect of international patent application filing. Normally, filing under the direct route or Paris Convention route leads to faster decisions regarding the granting of a patent. For companies in fast-moving sectors where product life cycles can be short, the company may consider it more important to be granted the patent more rapidly. In this situation, they may prefer to file directly rather than follow the PCT route.

Further comment – this is important

If you receive an unfavourable search report at month 16, you may decide to abandon your application. Timing is crucial here because the application will also be published 18 months after the original filing date.

This allows a two-month window to take action.

If you want to maintain your invention as a trade secret, you must take steps to withdraw the application before it is published for all your competitors to see.

It would be very unfortunate to have your application denied, patent protection disallowed, and still have your trade secret revealed to the world.

Chapter 8 – Trademarks

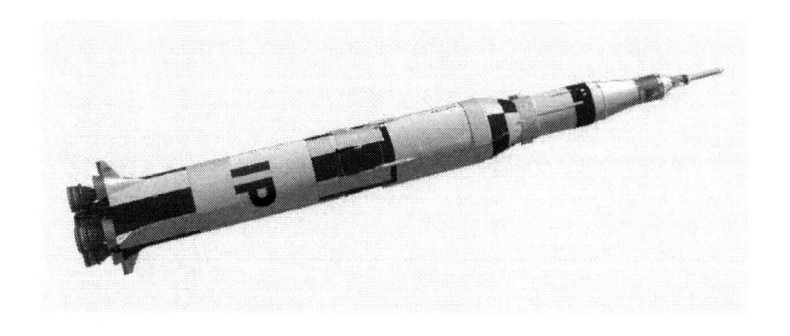

Trademarks in IP strategy

Patents and Copyright can be potent tools of technology companies. They allow you to build a market position without being copied by competitors. Companies can serve customers through protected, innovative offerings and excellent service. As they do this, they build a positive reputation in the market.

Trademarks are one more tool available in the IP strategy of a tech company. As you build your reputation and good name, you can protect this name and build it into something of value over the long term. Furthermore, a trademark has the possibility of continuing in existence even after the life of the patent protection has expired.

Types of trademark

Trademarks can be words, logos, slogans, names, symbols, shapes, colours, sounds and smells that manufacturers or service providers use to identify their products or services.

Application process

In the USA, you do not need to formally register a trademark. If you are the owner of a trademark, you can affix the mark "™" without registration. Ownership of a trademark can be established through usage. However, without registration, protection will be limited to the geographical market of use.

US federal registration strengthens the protection and brings additional benefits:

- Instead of the "™" mark, you are allowed (but not obliged) to attach the "®" mark to indicate your registration of the trademark.

- You are not allowed to attach this indicator if your trademark has not been registered formally.
- Registration means your trademark will be listed in the USPTO database.
- It indicates legal ownership and the exclusive right to use the trademark in the USA for the particular class(es) of product or service.
- Registration makes it easier to prove ownership and defend your rights in court.
- A USPTO registration can be used as the basis of an application for registration in international jurisdictions.

USA common law trademarks

Under common law in the USA, a trademark is created through mere usage. You are not required to register it to obtain protection. However, as mentioned above, federal registration strengthens the level of protection. Additionally, it provides the basis for further international applications within 6 months of the original USA filing.

Even if you have a common-law trademark in the USA, other people could file for their own trademark in other countries.

For example, there was a less erotic version of Playboy magazine in Japan for decades that had no connection with the original USA version. The USA Playboy publishers tried very hard to dislodge the Japanese lookalike but were unsuccessful because of the prior Japanese registration by the Japanese publishers. Even the Playboy Bunny girls were appropriated in Japan, and these days the bunny girl with bunny ears and a bow tie are just regarded in Japan as a titillating costume with no connection to the original Playboy brand.

The message is that if you want to protect a valuable brand internationally, you need to file a registration in your national trademark office and then file international applications under the Paris Convention within 6 months in all countries that will be important.

How about outside the USA?

Unlike the USA, international protection is generally available only upon formal registration. There are exceptions for "famous" or "well-known" non-registered trademarks but the standard of proving fame is very high.

In China, Ferrari learned an expensive lesson about this. China has a strict first-to-register trademark regime that also has an exception for famous trademarks. In 1995, the firm White Clouds Sporting Merchandise applied for a trademark in the shape of a horse for use in connection with sporting apparel. When the Chinese Trademark Office published the prospective trademark in 1996, Ferrari lodged a timely opposition appeal. They opposed the White Clouds application on the basis that the Ferrari rampant horse symbol was a well-known mark. In 2007, the Chinese court found that the registration of the name Ferrari was not tied to the world-famous horse figure and refused Ferrari's application after more than 10 years of appealing.

The salutary message to international owners of valuable trademarks is to register their rights formally and in a timely manner and not rely on their "well-known" status alone.

Registration

In Chapter 3, we described how trademark registrations are territorial and according to the class of product or service. The registration fees are payable in each territory and are higher if more classes must be protected.

If you envisage the trademark being applied to a range of products now and in the future, you may want to go to the expense of initially registering in many relevant classes. The example we gave in Chapter 3 concerned a high-end fashion brand with registrations in the areas of jewellery (class 14), leather luggage (class 18) and clothing and shoes (class 25). If the same brand wants to extend into the area of perfumes and perfumed candles in future, it will also need to register in classes 3 and 4, respectively.

The classes can only be specified at time of initial registration. They cannot be added at a future date. That is why some companies register more broadly initially and then abandon a few classes when the future business evolution does not carry products or services in all of the expected classes.

Furthermore, because registration is on a national or regional basis, the company has the option to maintain registrations in different classes in different jurisdictions.

Do you need a lawyer or attorney to file a trademark application?

The USPTO website (www.uspto,gov) allows you to file a trademark application without using an attorney, so it is possible to take a do-it-yourself approach and save attorney fees.

That said, there are advantages to using an attorney. One is that you can save yourself a lot of time and disappointment by first searching if there are similar pending or granted trademarks that would block your own registration. You can search using standard online search engines and the Trademark Electronic Search System (TESS) that is provided by the USPTO. An attorney has more search tools and is more adept at performing searches that could reveal problematic trademarks that the inexperienced searcher might not find.

Furthermore, within about 4 months of the application being filed, the patent office usually responds to the applicant with specific questions. You can respond to this set of questions, known as an "office action," but it is highly advisable that you use an experienced trademark attorney to handle correspondence at this stage. The responses to the office action will have an impact on the outcome of the application and could also influence the strength of the trademark in future legal actions.

International registration
Trademark protection is offered through registration in national or regional trademark offices. The most common way is to file an application in your home country and then file in your chosen international jurisdictions under the Paris Convention within 6 months of your original filing.

Chapter 9 – Trademark Strategies

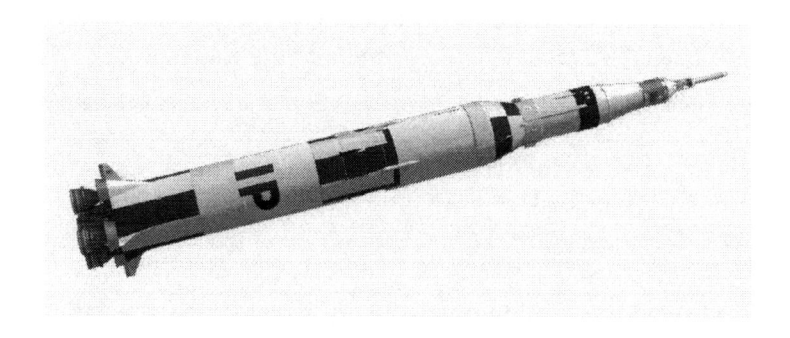

Maintenance

A trademark registration can continue in existence for as long as the trademark continues being used and registration renewal fees are paid in a timely manner, usually every 10 years.

Because fees are payable nationally and according to the number of classes, maintenance costs stack up. The company may decide that it no longer needs protection in certain classes in certain territories. They can simply cease paying renewal fees or elect to abandon their trademarks in that territory.

When a company has a large portfolio of trademarks with renewals falling due on different dates, it can become complex to maintain the registrations efficiently. If the company misses the deadline to pay renewal fees, the registration can be annulled. The company has the possibility in exceptional circumstances to apply to the trademark office within 6 months stating why the trademark should be reinstated. However, if they miss that opportunity, then they will lose the protection for that trademark and will not be able to revive it at a future date.

There are third-party firms that offer services that can look after reminders and even handle timely payments of fees. For less complicated portfolios, the maintenance can be scheduled and managed as an administrative task using even basic spreadsheet tools.

It is well known in the branding world that it is generally more expensive to create a new brand than it is to maintain an existing one. Even for companies like Polaroid, where the underlying business went bankrupt, there was enough nostalgia towards the original brand to allow it to be revived and the surviving trademark has significant value as an asset. This was only possible because the registration of the trademarks continued to be maintained during the difficult years.

Distinctiveness

Trademark protection is granted on the basis that the trademark is distinctive. If that distinctiveness becomes lost, the trademark can be annulled without any possibility of being revived.

For large organisations with valuable trademarks, this can be a serious consideration. Sometimes the loss of distinctiveness is through behaviours that are outside the control of the trademark owner. Xerox Corporation, for example, places full-page advertisements in trade magazines that are aimed at authors and professional writers. They request the authors to not use the word "Xerox" as a generic term for "photocopying" unless they really mean using a Xerox-made machine for copying.

This is not a trivial matter. The name "Escalator" was originally a trademark that was owned and exploited by the Otis Elevator Company until 1950. The term was found to be generic by the Examiner of Trademark Interferences, because most people understood the word to simply mean a moving staircase. The trademark office also cited casual language used by Otis themselves in other patent applications and advertising materials, so the protection was lost. Now all companies are free to use the word "escalator" in a generic way to describe their moving staircases.

Brand extension and dilution

Trademarks can underpin brands and can support premium value for products. It can be possible for a successful business to use their brand reputation to extend into other areas. For example, the affection people feel for the drink Coca Cola, has allowed them to capitalise on the brand and offer other branded merchandise to loyal fans. Coca Cola has a thriving business licensing merchandise such as backpacks, t-shirts, baseball caps and drinking bottles.

This opportunity to build on the value of a successful trademark can be an enticing prospect to generate income through introduction of new products or royalties from licensing fees.

However, there are risks associated with this too. Extending the brand into other areas that are not compatible with the original brand heritage can damage the reputation of the original brand. Furthermore, indiscriminate extensions into other areas could result in the original brand becoming "diluted" by being used in different applications. As mentioned above, one of the conditions of a trademark being awarded is that it must be distinctive. If the brand loses distinctiveness, the trademark faces the risk of being cancelled, just like Otis lost the protection of the Escalator trademark.

Evidence of use

Trademarks have a lifetime that is theoretically limitless provided they continue to be used and the registration fees are renewed as required. That condition of continuous use is important – trademark offices do not want to grant protection to a company who will block others from registering a potentially popular mark even though they have no intention of using the trademark themselves.

If an opposing player wishes to gain access to a trademark that is not in use, they can apply for the trademark to be revoked on grounds of non-use. The burden of proof in that situation is on the trademark owners to show that they have had more than "token use" of the trademark in the territory in the relevant classes during the previous 5 years.

In 2019, shockwaves reverberated throughout the trademark community when McDonald's had their European trademark "Big Mac" revoked because they failed to prove to the satisfaction of the EUIPO that they used the trademark in the European Community.

Most uninformed observers would think that such a prominent trademark as the Big Mac would be robust and unassailable. While McDonald's have appealed the decision, there are lessons to be learned by owners of valuable trademarks.

The main objective is to maintain evidence of use of products that can be relied on in the eventuality that there is ever a hostile attempt to revoke the trademark in future. After an action has been started by the trademark office, it is very difficult to go back and construct such evidence unless you have already gathered and stored it in anticipation of such a scenario.

Because trademarks are registered by country, and by classification, you should think of this exercise as one of completing a matrix that covers every country and every class of registration. For each element of the matrix, you should maintain evidence such as physical samples of the product with the trademark attached, product brochures with dates and countries identified, copies of sales notes and invoices of products specifying the trademark and quantities sold in each region.

While it can take considerable effort to set up such a body of evidence, maintaining it on a continuous basis is not so complicated. It is merely a matter of administrative discipline and routine. Indeed, the activity does not even have to be maintained by a trademark professional – the task lends itself to management by a dependable and meticulous office administrator.

Licensing opportunities and risks

Because a trademark is an asset, you have a range of options at your disposal when you want to exploit it. This can be through using it, trading it, selling it or licensing it.

Licensing is a way to generate income in the form of royalties while continuing to own the asset and allowing others access to the intellectual property under controlled conditions.

While licensing is an opportunity to generate other streams of income, there are potential risks associated that need to be managed.

Most of those risks can be controlled by the provisions of the licensing agreement and others can be managed through maintaining collaborative relationships with licensees.

Licensees should be selected carefully because their actions have the potential to damage the brand and the value of the trademark. The conditions of the licensing agreement must be arranged to ensure the licensee does not do anything that would undermine the value of the asset.

Chapter 10 – Trade secrets

What are trade secrets?

A trade secret can be a formula, pattern, device or anything else that is not known outside the company and has value because it is secret.

Can trade secrets be protected legally?

In international law, the three conditions for a trade secret are that:

1. it is not known outside the company;
2. it is of economic value because it is secret; and,
3. reasonable steps have been taken to protect secrecy.

Each of these elements has been explored and refined in legislation and litigation over the decades. For trade secrets to enjoy legal protection, companies must be able to identify their trade secrets and must take a proactive approach to protecting these assets as a part of a broader IP strategy.

Is a trade secret the same as "confidential information"?

Trade secrets can be considered a subset of confidential information. While trade secrets are confidential, some confidential information would not be regarded as a trade secret in a legal sense.

For example, the home phone number of a CEO can be confidential information. If this confidentiality is breached, the CEO would be distressed personally, but the company would not suffer materially, and competitors are unlikely to benefit economically from the information. This lack of *economic value* would disqualify such confidential information from being classified as a trade secret.

Should I mark everything as "Trade Secret"?

So, is the solution to stamp every document and communication as "secret" or "confidential"?

The answer is no.

Marking something as confidential delineates it as being special. Overly liberal labelling of every document as confidential dilutes the value of the ones that are actually sensitive.

And, as noted above, because all confidential items are not necessarily trade secrets, it makes more sense to mark the important secrets as "Trade Secret," especially in the light of increased awareness of trade secrets as a protectable asset.

Can trade secrets be patented?

In some ways, patents are the opposite of trade secrets. Patents are published and searchable, which makes the subject matter visible to anyone who wants to know. Trade secrets are not published and are hidden from view. So, a patent is not a trade secret.

However, trade secrets that are useful, novel and non-obvious may be amenable to patenting. If these trade secrets are to be incorporated into a product or service that could be reverse engineered, the secret will be exposed as soon as the product is put on the market. For such features, patenting is one route to consider as a protection mechanism for that element of the company's intellectual property.

In this way, many trade secrets can be seen as a precursor to patenting. Typically, a company that has several patents will also have built up a body of trade secrets.

Difficulties defending trade secrets in court

One of the problems when seeking help from a court to protect trade secrets is the public nature of court hearings.

This presents a dilemma.

When the judge asks about the trade secret, the company will be hesitant to reveal the secret in court. If the secret is not identified, the judge cannot rule on the question of misappropriation.

If the secret is revealed and the company prevails in the court case, the bad behaviour can be punished in respect of the single occurrence. So you win one case, but the public revelations will result in you as the trade secret owner losing the secrecy and thus the protection afforded to that particular trade secret against future misappropriation.

Hurdles to consider

Before taking a trade secret misappropriation action, you need to consider several aspects that are relevant to the case which will also be queried by the courts.

- Identifying the trade secret – All companies have knowhow, confidential information and trade secrets. It can be difficult to identify which of these qualifies as trade secrets, but it is important when relying on legislative protection.

- Establishing ownership – The plaintiff will have to demonstrate ownership of the trade secret.
- Evidence of misappropriation – It can be difficult to establish how the trade secret was misappropriated. In this digital age, trade secret misappropriation often involves the copying or removal of a large amount of data. This type of activity can leave traces, but it is important that any investigative activity does not compromise the trail of evidence that could be used in a court case.
- The accused bad actor – You will need to identify the person (or persons) involved in the activity, their behaviour and action, and how they used the trade secrets afterwards.
- Assessment of damages – Because trade secrets are valuable, you need to establish the value of those secrets, as well as prove what damages were caused to your company by the misappropriation or what advantage was gained by the receiver of the trade secrets.
- Your objective – What are you trying to achieve? Can financial compensation alone address the loss adequately? Is your intention to stop the further dissemination of your trade secrets? Do you want to "send a message" to discourage future activities that might lead further leakage of trade secrets?

Recent legislative developments in protection of trade secrets

Trade secret protection has evolved through legislation and court actions. In recent years, there has been active legislation in important jurisdictions. This new legislation highlights how important trade secrets are becoming as intangible assets, with a concomitant rise in awareness on the executive agenda.

USA – Defend Trade Secrets Act (2016)

The DTSA, signed into law by President Barack Obama, came into force in May 2016. Prior to the DTSA, companies could only sue for trade secret misappropriation in state courts. Different states had different definitions of "trade secret," different statutes of limitations and different remedies.

Now, companies can choose to sue in either a state or federal court.

One powerful tool of the DTSA is the civil seizure mechanism which allows courts to grant an order to seize equipment and materials to prevent propagation or dissemination of trade secrets during the pendency of a DTSA case.

European Union – Directive on Trade Secrets (2016)

The European Union Directive on Trade Secrets is based on a proposal from the European Commission and was adopted by the European Parliament and Council in June 2016. It came into force in the national legislation of all EU member states by June 2018.

The directive harmonises trade secret protection throughout the EU. The directive adopted a common definition of trade secrets in harmony with international standards, and prohibits unlawful acquisition, use or disclosure of trade secrets.

Civil remedies include.

- injunctions to prevent unlawful use and further disclosure.
- recall or destruction of infringing goods.
- payment of damages.

Japan – Unfair Competition Prevention Act (2018)

Japan first enacted the Unfair Competition Prevention Act in 1934 with its membership of the Paris Convention. At that time the focus was on preventing misleading source identification that could cause consumer confusion. Over the years this law was amended, and in 1990 it introduced trade secret protection.

Under this law, trade secrets were defined as being:

- useful for commercial activities such as manufacturing or marketing;
- kept secret; and,
- generally unknown to the public.

Following amendments, the Unfair Competition Prevention Act (UCPA) came to cover:

- improper acquisition of trade secrets;
- improper disclosure and misappropriation of trade secrets; and,
- interference with technology restrictions.

Because of the growing value of data, the UPCA was amended in 2018 to allow for civil penalties for the unfair acquisition, disclosure and use of data for limited disclosure.

It also provides for civil and criminal penalties for interference with technology restrictions, namely using machines or software to defeat digital rights management (DRM) controls.

This amendment came into effect on 1 July 2019.

China – Anti Unfair Competition Law

China originally enacted its Anti Unfair Competition Law in 1993. The first update to this law was in 2017, becoming effective in January 2018, and it was updated again in 2019.

The latest update expanded the scope from the original areas of "technical information" and "business operation information" to now include "commercial information" too. The new law also includes cyber theft.

Remedies are mainly civil except where there is evidence of serious losses. In the case of "exceptionally serious" losses, penalties can include a fine and/or a prison sentence of up to 7 years.

Comment

Clearly, trade secret protection is becoming a topic on the executive agenda. Major economies have all implemented or updates laws in the past three years.

The combination of civil and criminal remedies in some of these jurisdictions raises an interesting dimension. Apart from pure trade secret legislation, criminal sanctions can be very impactful.

In the USA, the Computer Fraud and Abuse Act covers unauthorised access to a protected computer. One of the biggest problems with trade secret theft is the speed of response. When a trade secret is in the form of data, you want to prevent it from being disseminated or destroyed. Normal civil remedies can take too long to work through the courts. This Act can be a powerful way to collect evidence before it could be destroyed. Furthermore, the threat of imprisonment can be very potent.

Another related piece of legislation is the Economic Espionage Act. This act allows for imprisonment of up to 10 years, and if the beneficiary is a foreign government, imprisonment can be up to 15 years.

Significance for senior executives

For senior executives of large organisations who might previously have been less scrupulous about their obligations regarding trade secrets, civil sanctions for infringement could be covered by absorbing the financial penalty and possibly reclaiming costs from insurance. In the new environment, if senior executives face the personal risk of spending time in prison. Such a high personal cost may cause them to be more prudent when considering misappropriating someone else's trade secrets.

These criminal sanctions add a further dimension of complexity in IP strategy and can help redress the balance of power when a growth-stage technology company is entering a potential David-versus-Goliath environment with enormous competitors, customers or development partners.

International reach

Most of this book describes how intellectual property rights such as patents, trademarks and copyright are protected under national legal systems. Generally, these rights are strictly geographical. They apply in each jurisdiction where they are protected, and enforcement is on a country-by-country basis.

An interesting aspect of trade secret protection is that it is not confined geographically in the same way as patents, trademarks and copyright. The US laws have extraterritorial reach. That is, you do not need to even be present on American soil to be accused of trade secret misappropriation in the USA and subject to extradition requests.

This same concept of extraterritorial reach is also present in trade secret legislation in other jurisdictions, which brings an international dimension to trade secret protection that is not available in other areas of IP protection.

Chapter 11 – Trade secret strategies

What are the advantages of trade secrets over patents?

On the face of it, there are several advantages of maintaining trade secrets over patents. As discussed in Chapter 4, there are several hurdles regarding eligibility, novelty and inventive step that have to be met before a patent can be granted. There can be a period of several years from patent application filing to formal granting. There are associated professional costs and official fees. And even then, the ultimate grant of the patent is by no means guaranteed.

Trade secrets do not have such potential impediments. There are no legal costs, application fees, registration fees or renewal fees.

One of the requirements for patent protection is that you must publish it. Trade secrets by definition are not published – publishing them would destroy the secrecy. This means that you do not need to show your hand to your competitors. It is always an important consideration when filing a patent application as to whether the benefits of protection outweigh the requirement to publish the invention for all to see.

A more disturbing variant on this analysis is the complication introduced by the possibility of invalidation. A patent gives the inventor the ability for a limited time (usually up to 20 years) to prevent others from using the invention. If the patent is revoked by a court on the basis that it was issued improperly by the patent office, the invention has been published already for all competitors to see without any residual benefit for the inventor. This publication requirement is a further reason why more companies are considering trade secrets as an alternative to seeking patent protection.

Even if the invalidation scenario does not arise, there is a finite limit to its life. When a patent expires, you cannot prevent anyone from using it. And don't forget that the initial publication will give competitors a detailed recipe for practising the idea themselves afterwards.

Conversely, there is no time limit on the life of a trade secret (for as long as you can keep it secret). Coca Cola is one of the most famous examples. The recipe was created by Dr John S. Pemberton in 1886 and was not even written down at that time. The formula was committed to paper in 1919 as collateral for investment and stored in a bank vault. Some 130 years later, the trade secret continues to survive, even though some people occasionally claim to have reverse engineered it and published the "recipe" on the internet.

What are the drawbacks of trade secrets?

While there is an attractiveness to avoiding the inconvenience and cost of filing patent applications, trade secrets are not necessarily "free." There can be a high cost to protect the secrecy, especially when employees are involved. You may have to pay higher salaries to employees to ensure they maintain confidentiality. You will have to institute security controls to limit access to secret information.

Collaborations with external parties may also be troublesome. In an age where more open collaboration is encouraged, it may be challenging to get other parties to commit to non-disclosure agreements. The time spent in negotiating the NDA delays the ability to start new projects and establish ad-hoc project groups. And some potential collaborators may simply refuse absolutely to sign an NDA.

Long-term employees naturally build up a lot of valuable knowledge. When they leave the company, they carry that knowledge in their heads.

Do you remember in Chapter 1 how trade secrets are defined? There are 3 elements to trade secrets:

1) They must not be generally known to other people;
2) They must have either value to you or could damage you if others got to know them; and,
3) You must take active steps to protect the secrecy.

If you ever have to rely on the protection of the courts from loss of trade secrets, you will have to produce evidence of all three points.

Most companies are conscious of the first two elements. They concern the definition of the secrecy of a trade secret. The third element concerns the conduct of the owner of the trade secrets. Mere passive protection is not enough when seeking trade secrets protection in a court. The company must take <u>active</u> steps to protect its secrets and needs to document these steps in a way that can be used as evidence if it is ever required in a legal setting.

The good news is that many of the ways of protecting trade secrets are simply a matter of common sense and good operating practices.

Ways of protecting trade secrets

As noted, there is an obligation on the owner to take reasonable steps to protect the secrecy of trade secrets. For the steps to be considered "reasonable," the company should follow a multi-faceted approach. These initiatives can be in the form of legal, physical, technological protections and operating disciplines.

Legal

Non-disclosure agreements should always be put in place and executed before any trade secrets are exposed to third parties such as customers, suppliers, outsourcing partners, and investors. These agreements should put an obligation on those partners to maintain the protection of trade secrets and ensure they control the behaviour of their own employees in this respect.

One of the biggest risks of trade secret leakage comes from your own employees. Whether it comes from an existing employee who is offered financial enticement to divulge secrets, a disgruntled employee who wants to exact revenge, or a former employee who takes secrets when going to join a new employer. Employment agreements should include clauses to ensure that employees understand the importance of protecting the company's secrets. Furthermore, those agreements should have clear clauses that state the confidentiality obligations will continue to remain in force even after the employment is ended.

Physical

Another facet of trade secret protection is physical protections. Building security should be arranged in such a way that there can be no unauthorised access by strangers to trade secrets. This physical protection can be in the form of locked doors, security barriers, and electronic access control limited to authorised employees. When visitors arrive, they should be accompanied by employees and not allowed to wander unaccompanied into sensitive areas.

Old-fashioned measures such as frosted glass windows and safes are still very effective. Sensitive documents and models can be locked in storage cabinets or filing cabinets.

Technological

Technological measures are effective in protecting sensitive data and electronic documents. Computers should be protected against viruses and unauthorised access.

With the proliferation of mobile devices these days, it is common to hear about laptops or smartphones being lost or stolen, sometimes containing valuable and confidential data. These devices should be protected with the appropriate level of encryption and have the ability to have their data erased remotely when one is lost or stolen.

Operating disciplines

The legal, technological and physical protections above can be rendered ineffective by sloppy operational execution. Even with NDAs and confidentiality agreements in place, management should reinforce behaviour through communications and company-wide training to maintain disciplines.

Human memories fail and bad habits can set in. Employees and third parties need to be reminded from time to time about their obligations.

Even when all employees are covered by agreements and confidentiality obligations, it is good practice to limit access to critical information on a need-to-know basis. Broadcasting confidential information indiscriminately to large numbers of employees carries increasing risk of leakage. Companies that do not limit the circulation of information may have difficulty relying on the protection of the courts in a future trade secret litigation action.

When employees are departing, the exit interview and termination documents should remind the employee that their confidentiality obligations continue after the end of their employment.

Physical access controls can be defeated if an employee fails to lock the door or politely encourages "tailgating" by holding the door open when someone is following into a secure area.

Other simple disciplines can be to encourage clean-desk policies and ensure that employees erase the white board when a meeting is finished.

Before visitors arrive, sensitive information should be put away or covered up. It is good discipline to assign non-identifiable project names and avoid having customer names on display when outsiders arrive on a visit.

Innovative companies these days encourage employees to be active on social media and some employees may have their own blogs. These activities support free thinking and employee empowerment. They also can foster engagement with the wider innovation community.

With this increased openness and ability to disseminate information, there is the concomitant risk of leakage of confidential information and trade secrets. Bearing these risks in mind, the company should have easily understood policies on social media use and what employees may publish.

IP strategy – when is it better to file a patent rather than protect with a trade secret?

The focus of the chapters on trade secrets is to emphasise the option of trade secrets as an integral element of an IP strategy. At some stage the Invention Review Board (IRB) must make a decision whether to file a patent for a certain invention or keep it as a trade secret.

This chapter has already highlighted some of the advantages of trade secrets. Some of these are listed here:

- Trade secrets don't need to have the same level of novelty or inventiveness as a patent.
- There are no filing fees.
- The content does not have to be published.
- There is no expiry of the trade secret for as long as the secrecy remains protected, so it has a theoretically infinite life.

Apart from these considerations, the IRB will need to balance questions about reverse engineering, detectability and other strategic reasons outlined in the next section.

Will the technology appear in a product on the market that could be identified by reverse engineering?
If the product appears on the market with visible technological features, those features will need to be protected before the public gains access. Even releasing the product or brochures can become viewed as prior art that would invalidate any subsequent patent application.

If the technology is in the form of some secret manufacturing knowhow that goes into the making of the product but is not visible in the final product, this might be a candidate for trade secret protection rather than patent protection.

However, if the knowhow could be inferred by reverse engineering, a patent is a better way of protecting it.

Infringement detectability

The corollary of the previous concept relates to the ability to detect potential infringement. If the technology refers to manufacturing process knowhow that cannot be inferred from the finished product, this creates an additional problem. Even if a competitor copies your process, you may not be able to detect the infringement or prove it in subsequent litigation, especially if you do not have access to their manufacturing facilities.

In such a situation, patent protection cannot be relied upon because you will not be able to enforce your rights. In such a situation, you do not want to register a patent that requires you to disclose that kind of knowhow to potential competitors.

Such knowhow would be more amenable to protection as a trade secret.

Strategic reasons for filing a patent on a trade secret

Notwithstanding the previous considerations, there are strategic reasons for converting a trade secret into a patent application. If a competitor comes up with the knowhow independently and files a patent to protect it, you cannot rely on the fact that you had this trade secret for many years as grounds to attack their patent application. Because your trade secret was not published externally (after all, it is a secret), it cannot be used as prior art to block someone else's patent application.

If you are in a highly competitive field, where it is possible that one or more competitors are working on the same technical challenges, there may be a strategic benefit to filing a patent application pre-emptively so as to prevent others from filing a patent application that could result in you being blocked from practising your own trade secret.

Chapter 12 – Recognising intangibles in accounting terms

The bulk of this book covers the most common forms of IP that are relevant to tech CEOs. We have paid attention to patents, trademarks and trade secrets. We have examined how to capture and protect these rights, and some strategies for exploitation.

The focus has been on protection and exploitation which are key elements of IP strategy. A further benefit of pursuing these activities lies in the way these assets can contribute towards enhancing the intangible value of a company that can be recognised in accounting terms.

While traditional accounting very often disregards the value of intangible assets other than the original cost of creation, accounting standards do allow for intangible value to be recognised.

This means that the accounting information may not be suited entirely for making management evaluations and decisions about key intangible assets.

If, for example, a trademark has a value of $1 million to the business but the legal costs of creation and maintenance were $20,000, the recorded value of $20,000 does not tell the complete story. Similarly, there are portfolios of patents that may have cost hundreds of thousands of dollars to register and maintain but technological obsolescence can mean the underlying technology is no longer relevant or contributing to future business value.

Clearly it is not useful to record high-value assets simply at mere cost of development. Similarly, it is inaccurate to maintain obsolete assets on your books without impairing them for accounting purposes. These two "wrongs" do not balance out to give a "right" picture. However, that is the way that IP is often valued in traditional accounts.

Two levels of measurement

This chapter will deal briefly with two levels of measurement of intangible value:

- Traditional accounting rules for intangibles
- Intellectual capital accounting

IAS 38

As mentioned, accounting standards do allow somewhat for the valuation of intangibles.

International accounting standard IAS 38 deals specifically with accounting for intangibles. While all accounting students learn about this as part of their professional formation, very few ever get to grips with this standard on a practical level in their subsequent careers. Even though this tool is at their disposal, it is common for the relevant to be expensed in the P&L rather than accumulating assets in the balance sheet.

Under IAS 38, intangible assets are defined as assets, other than financial assets, with no physical form. There are three conditions for intangibles to be recognised under IAS 38. They must be:

1) identifiable;
2) controllable (as the result of a past event, such as being acquired or created); and,
3) able to lead to future economic benefits (usually as income or reduced costs)

There are two conditions for an asset to be regarded as "Identifiable." It must:

- be separable – it can be separated and then sold, transferred, licensed, rented or exchanged; and,
- arise from contractual or legal rights.

Some examples of intangible assets are patents, trademarks, customer lists, territorial market approvals, etc.

In accounting terms, an asset must be recognised as an expense unless it (a) satisfies the definition of an intangible asset, (b) there are probable future economic benefits, and (c) the cost can be reliably measured.

If the intangible asset is covered in another standard, it cannot be counted as an asset under IAS 38. Some examples of excluded assets are assets for sale (under IFRS 5), deferred taxes, goodwill and financial assets (IAS 32 and IFRS 9), and exploration and evaluation assets (IFRS 6).

Does R&D come under IAS 38?

The answer depends on whether you focus on research or on development.

Einstein has been quoted as saying, "If we knew what we were looking for, we wouldn't call it Research, would we?" Research in its most general form is an investigative activity without a certain outcome. While pure research may advance scientific understanding, it is not focussed on generating products directly. This lack of a link to probable future economic benefit means that research activity should be expensed rather than be treated as an asset under IAS 38.

Development, on the other hand, can be considered an asset if, on subsequent analysis, it satisfies the following conditions:

- There are probable future economic benefits;
- You have the intention to complete the development and use or sell the results;
- Resources (technical, financial, etc.) are adequate to develop and then commercially use or sell the results;
- You are able to use or sell the results;
- It is technically feasible; and,
- Expenditures can be measured reliably.

What about Goodwill?

Goodwill acquired in a business combination comes under IFRS 3 and is therefore outside IAS 38.

Internally-generated goodwill comes within the scope of IAS 38 but is not recognised as an intangible asset because it is not an identifiable/separable resource.

For the same reason, internally generated brands, mastheads and customer lists are not recognised as assets under IAS 38.

Cost model or revaluation model?

Initially, qualifying intangible assets are valued at cost.

The revaluation model is based on the arm's-length value of the asset if there is an active market. Some examples of active markets are the markets for taxi licenses or pub licenses.

If the asset is revalued, its value must be recalculated at the end of each accounting period – usually at financial year end. If the asset has a finite life, the value will be amortised and the annual accounts will reflect the amortisation cost less any revaluation adjustment.

The amortisation calculation should reflect the pattern of useful benefits from the asset. If there is no definite pattern, straight-line amortisation should be applied.

If an asset is accounted for with the revaluation model rather than the cost model, all other assets in the same class must be accounted for in the same way unless there is no active market for those assets.

As a further observation, if a previously active market no longer exists when performing periodic revaluations, it can be an indication that the asset could be impaired and may need to be tested in accordance with IAS 36 – impairment of assets.

Intellectual capital accounting

If you apply the accounting methodologies reviewed in this chapter, you have the possibility of recognising intangible assets and their potential future contribution to the business.

However, these traditional methodologies still do not provide a comprehensive overview of the full value of a high-growth technology business.

Traditional accounting rules are grounded in business models that sprung from the era of the industrial revolution. If you compare two software companies purely on the basis of office square footage and investment in office equipment, you will not be able to get a reliable way of deciding which one has the most valuable intangible assets and greatest potential for innovative breakthroughs.

The previous section on recognising valuable intangibles for accounting purposes is limited in scope because it focuses mainly on structural intangibles such as patents, trademarks and trade secrets.

In Chapter 3, we mentioned that intellectual capital is made up of three elements. Apart from structural capital (the focus of this book), there are: human capital (including the knowledge inside the heads of employees), and relational capital (such as customer relationships, supply chain relationships and customer loyalty).

Tesla, the automotive company, is worth more than the sum of its patents. Clearly, investors have placed a lot of trust in its charismatic CEO, Elon Musk, and the abilities of the team he has assembled. Furthermore, the fierce loyalty of its customers has added to the perceived value of the brand and confidence for the company's future.

When Chief Design Officer Jony Ive announced recently that he would be leaving Apple, there was a flurry of analysis by business commentators on TV, in newspapers and online. The share price fell 1.5% to $197.44 – a drop of around $9 billion in value – in a single day.

Is one man really worth $9 billion?

Despite the initial fear that the departure of such an iconic contributor would have a heavy impact on the wellbeing of the company, there was a very quick consensus that thousands of Apple employees have absorbed Mr. Ives' messages about functionality, elegance and simplicity of product design, and that his legacy would continue after his departure.

By the end of the day, Apple's share price had recovered almost completely to close at $199.74. In the following day of trading, the price continued rising, as if nothing had ever happened.

If "the most important assets are our people," why aren't they recognised on our balance sheet?

There is a saying that "what gets measured gets managed." If innovation is the goal, why is accounting still focussed on recording land, buildings and machines?

This book encourages a more comprehensive application of existing accounting rules to generate a picture that recognises the contribution of structural intangibles to a business.

If you want to get a more detailed picture of your company's intangible value, you can create a supplementary "balance sheet" of intellectual capital. This balance sheet records debits and credits in the intangible account in a more comprehensive way than traditional accounting.

While this balance sheet cannot be recognised in the formal financial accounts of the company, it is very useful to track the evolution of intangible value. It provides a practical way to record a baseline and then chart the progress or decline of the company's value.

When a company can demonstrate how its intangible assets really contribute to value, investors can make decisions about how they will commit to further investment in developing innovative capacity.

Comment

This chapter does not go into depth regarding methodologies. It is merely to show the CEO that there are valid ways to recognise assets that come from significant investments in developing intangibles and to encourage the CFO to pursue the topic in more detail.

Apart from more extensive use of existing accounting rules, the company can demonstrate control of its innovative destiny through growth in the value of the intellectual capital balance sheet.

Epilogue – IP strategy evolution

How does it all come together?

While every organisation has its own characteristics, IP strategy evolution in technology companies follows a typical process that moves through several stages that are tied closely to the RACER process described in Chapter 1.

Recognition
- Realising that there are IP gaps and "something" must be done

Audit
- Reviewing the status quo and establishing a baseline for improvement

Concrete Action Plan
- Identifying steps to be taken to address intangible gaps

Execution
- Mitigating IP risks and building intangible value

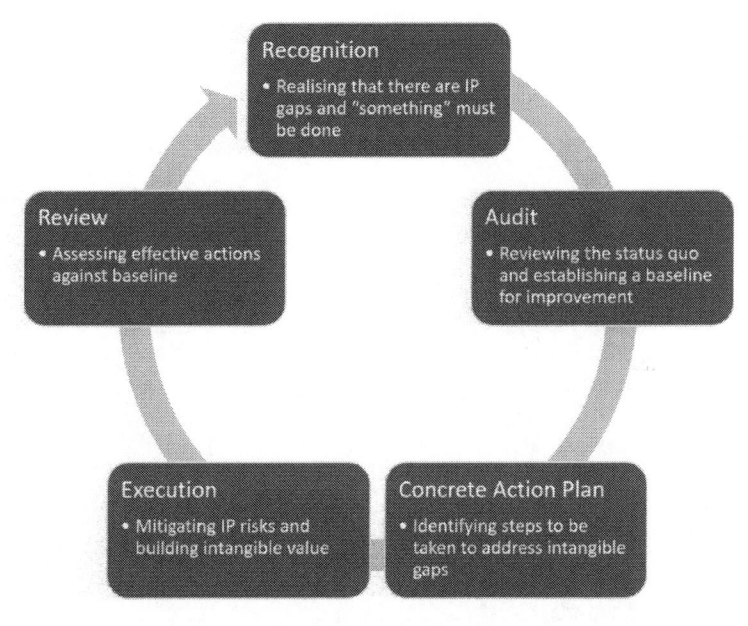

Review
- Assessing effective actions against baseline

Fig 7: RACER Cycle

You will recall that the process goes through the steps of recognition, audit, concrete action plan, execution and review. That process continues in a cycle that leads to ever-increasing sophistication in IP strategy and intangible value creation.

In practical terms, a technology company that follows a RACER cycle will move through seven levels of sophistication in IP strategy as outlined in the following diagram.

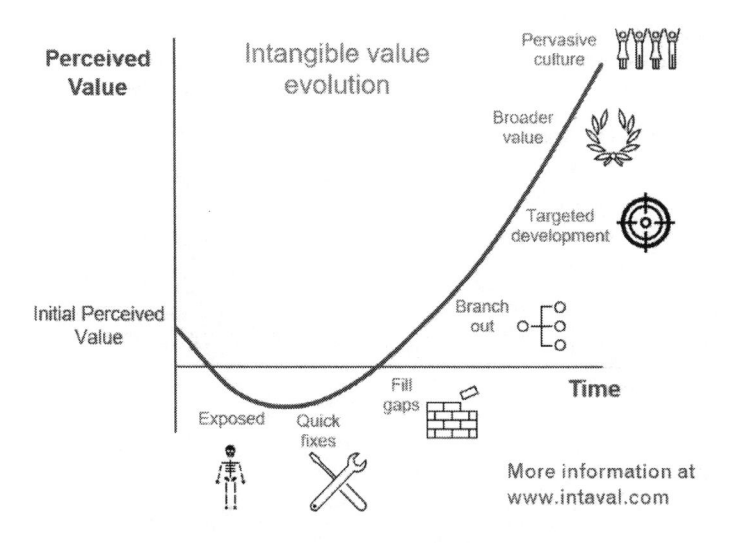

Fig 8: Intangible Value Evolution

Stage 1: Exposed

"The best time to plant a tree is 20 years ago. The second-best time is now." Apparently, this is wrongly attributed as a Chinese proverb. Nonetheless, its wisdom applies to IP strategy. There is no embarrassment in admitting a gap in IP. You simply have to start sometime.

In 2013, venture capitalist Aileen Lee used the term "Unicorn" to describe the rare companies that are privately held and have a valuation in excess of $1 billion. In 2015, there were 151 unicorns globally, of which 95 were based in the USA. These included companies such as Uber and AirBnb.

Naturally, one would think that such companies, with such a high part of their valuation being attributed to intangible value, would all have sophisticated IP strategies and strong patent portfolios. Foresight Valuation Group analysed published data on these 95 USA unicorns and found that 30% had no patents (issued or pending) at all and 62% had 10 or fewer patents (issued or pending).

Clearly, even companies with very high profiles can start with a significant IP deficit. The real power comes from recognising that this gap creates high risk for the business and realising that something must be done now.

Stage 2: Quick Fix

The Audit section of the RACER framework will highlight deficiencies that were previously invisible. This may be daunting and startling.

The positive news is that early audit findings can disclose areas where quick wins are possible. Reviewing contracts can highlight inconsistencies in protection. Does every employee have an employment contract? Are the terms consistent? Do they cover confidentiality? Do they cover ownership of employee-created IP? Are departing employees reminded in exit interviews that their confidentiality obligations continue after the employment is terminated?

Other contracts with suppliers and customers may also need to be tightened up on protection of confidentiality and ownership of IP. These contracts may also indicate obligations on the company in this regard.

If open-source software is being used, are there protections to ensure employees are not infringing on the IP of others? Even before looking at existing software for potential exposures, it is important to ensure that, going forward, all employees are aware of the requirement to not use code for any future development that could create new risks of infringing others' patents or copyright.

These initial measures can create immediate benefits and put the company on the path to increased value from IP strategy.

Stage 3: Fill Gaps

After the initial fixes outlined above, the next step is to fill gaps in protection using a program of invention mining to benefit from previous development work performed by the company. Any successful technology organisation will have had challenges in the past and will have tried to solve them with a variety of technological solutions that may have current applications.

Invention mining will identify the most promising technological candidates to take through a process of patent drafting that leads to patent applications being filed. This is a very effective way of filling the gaps in IP protection and building a relevant portfolio.

Until the patent application has been granted, it cannot be enforced. However, the priority date of the patent goes back to the application date. In other words, once a patent application is filed, the inventor does not need to have very restrictive non-disclosure agreements in place when discussing the technology from the point of view of disclosures that could invalidate their patent.

Another way to fill the gap is to acquire an issued patent that is available on the market. While it is not your own invention, there are some benefits to this strategy:

- You can skip the long timeline of waiting several years for a patent to be granted.
- You can de-risk the process because you can avoid the risk of a patent application not being granted.
- You can choose from a broad range of patents that are already in the market.
- You can select technologies that have been established for a few years.

While issued patents can be more expensive than filing for your own inventions, they do have the benefits of speed and increased certainty as outlined.

If you are facing into a competitive situation where you may need patents as weapons in future battles. If you are concerned about cash-flow considerations, you may be able to negotiate an exclusive option to purchase the patent by paying around 10-20% of the purchase price. This means you can avoid a large up-front expense and exercise the option to buy the patent only if it becomes necessary at some time in the future.

Stage 4: Branch out

While the early part of this book focuses on patents, a broader IP strategy will cover more than patents. As the

RACER process progresses and the business starts to show the fruits of IP-related activities, more people within the organisation become conscious of opportunities and the contribution of IP strategy to the company's business and the development of intangible value.

This consciousness allows strategy to branch out and extend past simple patenting activity into other forms of intangible value capture and exploitation such as trade secrets and trademarks.

Any company that has built a pipeline of patentable technologies will also have accumulated a broad base of knowhow and trade secrets. As we outlined in the chapters on Trade Secrets, recent legislation has further strengthened the protections for trade secrets. As employees become more aware of the value of trade secrets, they can take active steps to protect these valuable intangible assets.

Patents are excellent tools to protect an inventor and give the company time to build a business from the invention. This protection allows the company to develop a market, nurture its reputation, and deliver premium products to customers. The benefits of building this reputation can be further locked in with trademark protection that can continue in perpetuity even after the underlying patent may have expired.

This multi-faceted approach to the protection of intangible value reinforces and strengthens the overall strategic position.

Stage 5: Targeted Development

As awareness grows and as the gaps are filled, the company cycles through successive iterations of the RACER process. It can move on from opportunistic patenting activities and can focus on a deliberate strategy of intangible value creation.

Invention mining in the Fill the Gaps stage focuses on extracting value from historical development activities, capturing, protecting and building a base for exploitation. It looks at inventions from the past that may have current applicability.

As the company moves through the stages of IP strategy evolution, the focus moves from the past (protecting legacy inventions) to the future (targeted invention for future value).

Invention mining activity in the earlier stage of filling gaps points to a way to generate more intangible assets in the future. As the company generates a technology roadmap, it can start to plan development activities proactively and focus invention and patenting activity in areas that demonstrate the greatest promise of delivering future value.

Stage 6: Broader Value

The previous chapter outlined how intangible value can be recognised more concretely in financial terms. As the CFO becomes more familiar with how the company can account for intangible value, the return on investment in IP can be measured in financial terms.

This evolution in the company's IP sophistication and its intangible value creation is a story that will appeal to investors. It outlines, in financial terms that they can understand, how the proactive activities of the company generate intangible value that can be reflected in the balance sheet of the company.

If the company can introduce a supplementary way of tracking its "intellectual capital balance sheet," it can proactively control the evolution of the broader intangible value. Moreover, this track record can be used as evidence to demonstrate to investors how it is able to cover IP risks and build intangible value.

Investors will have more confidence committing funding to activities that can show continuing evolution and growth in intangible value.

Stage 7: Pervasive Culture

One benefit that is often overlooked is the increased level of engagement by employees and their sense of ownership around innovation.

Patent filing activity enables employees who have participated in innovative development to be recognised formally as named inventors on patents, highlighting their contribution to key drivers of the company's technological advancement. This recognition can be a spur to other employees to come forward with their own invention disclosures.

Heightened awareness of the importance of intellectual property will highlight the ways the company brings unique and special benefits to its market.

Multi-faceted recognition of intangibles as patents, trade secrets or trademarks support a culture of pride in how the company contributes to broader society.

All of this combines to give a stronger sense of purpose to employees and makes them highly engaged. These motivated employees will then contribute to generating sustainable, profitable results.

In an era when knowledge has value, companies are turning attention to identifying who has knowledge. From there, the company can follow a process of capturing, storing and making the knowledge reusable. In this way, the intangible value can be multiplied when made available to other team members and, furthermore, it will not be lost completely if an employee leaves the company.

IP risk management

While most of this book has described how to build and manage intangible value, it has touched on aspects of IP risk at various points. When so much value in high-growth technology companies is attributed to intangibles, this also means that intangible risks need to be managed.

As a company is building its value, its management will also need to pay attention to IP governance and ensure that management of IP risk is on the agenda.

IP risk management concerns the preservation of value and being ready to address threats. Some of those threats can be averted or mitigated by preventative measures. Some will arise as unforeseen IP emergencies. Even in the case of such emergencies, a well-prepared company will handle unexpected events in an organised fashion.

Examples of IP risks

Throughout the book, there are examples of IP risks in patents, trademarks and trade secrets.

In this modern era, data is often a critical asset. Typical IT system design is focused on data integrity. It will cover material business risks such as data corruption or loss. Systems are designed to withstand external threats such as breaches by hackers who will steal data, damage databases or activate ransomware. One additional vulnerability that should receive attention by IT system designers is the internal threat – deliberate sabotage by a disgruntled employee or theft of data by a departing employee.

Often, a well-managed company can be surprised to find that its subsidiaries and foreign entities do not have the same attitude to risk management as the parent company. While an IP audit may yield a healthy report for the headquarters, it may reveal a more exposed landscape for other offices and foreign locations.

With more global collaborations and open innovation programmes, third-party IP risks come into focus. While your own company may have strong protections around formal IP and trade secrets your supply chain may contribute to various vulnerabilities. Unless you manage these effectively, you could face supply chain disruption, reputational damage and unexpected legal costs. In this environment, you have to perform due diligence to identify and mitigate these external IP risks.

Just like you work with your suppliers to evaluate their financial strength, quality systems, environmental impact and worker safety, you can also help them to enhance overall IP protection. Modern supply chain management principles involve training suppliers and working with them on a shared responsibility and shared benefit.

In this way, IP risk management does not need to exist as a separate activity and can be combined with other activities in global management systems of policies procedures and records that cover areas including finance, quality, safety and reputation.

IP risk management steps

When a threat materialises, management should not be transfixed with panic or get caught debating what course of action to take. With prudent risk management, the pre-designed procedures and systems should be able to spring into action to handle the situation as it arises.

IP risk management is similar to general risk management in business and can be addressed in 5 steps, namely identify-analyse-mitigate-document-review.

- Identify – review the business and generate a list of potential IP risks
- Analyse – for each of the risks, assess the probability of the risk occurring and the impact if such a risk were to materialise. This analysis does not need to be very precise. For example, rather than assigning

an exact figure to the probability, they could be assessed as high, medium or low (or red, orange and green). Similarly, the impact can also be categorised as high, medium or low. The combination of probability and impact can then allow the mitigation measures to be prioritised.

- Mitigate – take steps to prevent avoidable risks and establish procedures to deal with IP risks as they materialise.
- Document – keep a record of IP risks as they materialise, the actions taken to mitigate them, and the outcomes experienced.
- Review – frequently analyse how IP risks actually materialise to assess the initial identification and analysis of potential IP risks, their probability and their impact. Also assess the effectiveness of mitigation activities on the actual outcomes. Use this assessment to fine-tune the company's readiness to handle IP risk on an ongoing business.

International standards

While it might appear that IP risk management is an activity that consumes valuable corporate resources, this activity can be part of a broader business risk management regime.

International standard ISO 31000 provides guidelines for risk management in organisations. While this standard cannot be used for certification purposes, it can help companies provide a framework to identify threats and opportunities and point to a system for managing risks.

The European Innovation Management Standard CEN/TS 16555 has been under development since 2008 and Part 4 deals specifically with Intellectual Property Management (16555-4:2018).

There is a German standard DIN 77006 which is a guideline for quality in intellectual property management. This is evolving and could eventually become an international standard.

The last word

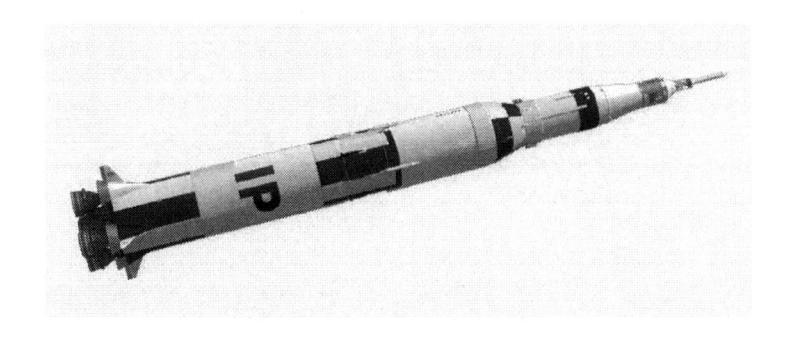

For people so inclined, there is no "last word" on IP strategy. For me, it is a lifetime of fascination and learning. I believe it will continue to be so.

I took a deliberate decision to keep this book as short as possible to give an overview of key areas of importance to CEOS of growth-stage technology companies. Indeed, any chapter in this book could be expanded to a three-day seminar and still just address the fundamentals.

I hope it has given you enough information to allow you to ask the right questions that will ensure that your IP strategy is aligned with your corporate strategy to drive your company's intangible value.

If you would like to explore any aspect in greater detail, please feel free to check out the IntaVal website (www.intaval.com) or send an email to coach@intaval.com.

Thank you and good luck on your journey.

Author Profile

Raymond Hegarty is an IP strategist who has studied in Ireland and France. He has a bachelor's degree in electronic engineering, an MBA, a master's degree in medical AI, a postgraduate diploma in European law and a master's degree in IP law.

He has built IP-intensive businesses in Japan, Ireland and Luxembourg, assembled & developed teams and implemented processes & systems for exploitation of IP. He has executed several billion dollars of patent and trademark transactions and has managed international commercialisation of a portfolio of 40,000 patents.

Mr Hegarty is the best-selling author of three books on IP strategy. He has advised the European Commission, the OECD and policy makers in several countries on national and international innovation strategies.

He currently advises CEOs of fast-growing technology and life science companies on IP strategy, is a regular conference speaker and is connected to the global professional IP community. He has been recognized by IAM Magazine since 2011 as one of the world's "Top 300 IP Strategists."

Printed in Great Britain
by Amazon

a6403b5b-56a5-4e47-9477-94cb3a76be00R01